A WORD FOR YOUR MIND, SPIRIT AND SOUL—
FOR EVERYDAY OF THE YEAR

DEVOTIONS

YOLANDA MARSHALL

Glimpse of Glory Christian Book Publishing
P O Box 94131
Birmingham, Al 35220

Unless otherwise noted Scriptures are taken from King James Version Bible.

ISBN: 978-0-983-32211-5

Printed in the United States of America

INTRODUCTION

"This is the day which the Lord hath made; we will rejoice and be glad in it." Did you know that God wants to say something to you every day? If you open your ears, heart and mind, you can receive a Word from the Lord everyday this year for your soul. Isn't that amazing? I realize that sometimes we may face different circumstances in our lives, and all we need is just one Word—until God gives us a fresh, new Word. The Word of God is so powerful and encouraging, and it will sustain us through everything.

I believe that you can learn how to apply something positive to your life everyday through this book. There are times in our lives when we just need to hear someone say, "I love you; God loves you more, be strong, I do care, hold fast and wait on the Lord, it is okay, you were born with a purpose, keep looking toward Heaven, and you will make it."

Well, God has allowed me to share these words through this book, so hold your head up and get ready to receive your daily blessings. You are going to experience something great each day of this year. Remember, "All things are possible with God."

JANUARY 1

GIVE THANKS TO GOD

I thank my God...

1Corinthians 14:18

This is the first day of the year. You should be smiling from ear to ear because God has blessed you to not only see another day, but He has also blessed you to see another year. Just stop what you are doing right now and give Him thanks. You can shout right where you are. The master saw fit to breathe on you today. Think about it. You can see the beauty of his nature. You can get in your car and drive to the grocery store, work or school. You can talk. You can hear. Why wouldn't you want to thank the One who made all of this possible?

He has so much He wants to reveal to you this year. So, go ahead and thank Him in advance for what He is about to do in your life. You will be amazed of His many blessings as you travel down Victorious Street. This will be a beautiful journey that you will enjoy, and it starts today.

JANUARY 2

THANK GOD THAT YOU HAVE THE VICTORY

But thanks be to God, which giveth us the victory through our Lord Jesus Christ.

1 Corinthians 15:57

We all had the victory from the moment our Lord, Jesus Christ, was raised from His grave. He showed us that we all can live a victorious life. We do not have to continue being afraid to live and serve our Heavenly Father. We are going to face some things in life, but we now know that we are true overcomers.

Therefore, you can laugh at the devil. You can boldly say that you have the victory. Let's thank God together for what He has already done in our lives, and what He will do for each of us today.

JANUARY 3

DON'T DOUBT GOD

I will therefore that men pray everywhere, lifting up holy hands, without wrath and doubting.

Timothy 2:8

You know, God is the only One we need to put full confidence, faith and trust in. That settles it. All mankind will put you down, so it is not uncommon to doubt people. But one thing's for certain, God won't let you down. You can bank on that. You do not want to doubt Him.

If you are struggling with doubting God, I want to encourage you to leave it at His feet. Don't pick it up, my brother. Stop worrying, my sister. What is the point of going to God in prayer if you are not going with an open, trusting, and receptive heart? You have to have faith and believe He is going to answer your prayers.

JANUARY 4

MAKE SURE YOU PRODUCE GOOD FRUIT

Even so every good tree bringeth forth good fruit...

Matthew 7:17

Today, make sure you produce healthy, good fruit. You might want to start examining how things are going from the moment you step foot out of your bed. Remember that you have an enemy that wants you to have a bad day. But you need to start your day by thanking God, saying a prayer and immediately declaring that you will have a good day. When you do these things, it will open the door for you to produce good fruit.

You will be able to treat everyone right, even your co-workers and your boss. I say this because some of you reading this book now have a problem with your boss, and some of your co-workers as well. For those of you who might not have a job, there is still something that can stand in the way of you producing good fruit, too. Remember, God is looking for people who are not going to let anyone or anything stand in the way of them producing good fruit. This is something that we should practice doing every day.

JANUARY 5

GET POWER THROUGH PRAYER

Pray without ceasing.

1 Thessalonians 5:17

Child of God, I want to tell you don't stop praying. You will find in the Word of God that the more Jesus prayed the more power He had. Did you know that the more you pray the more power you can receive, too? I realize that when I pray more, I tend to have more power to overcome obstacles. The power to stand still! The power to help others! The power to cast out devils! The power to see things change! This kind of power only comes through the Most High, Almighty God. None of us can do anything without Him.

You should try praying to God every time you think about it. If you are sitting at home right now, just stop and pray. If you are at work, just step away on your break and pray. If you are in the doctor's office, just take a moment to pray. You can commit to praying wherever you are today.

JANUARY 6

STOP WAVERING, JUST STICK WITH THE WORD OF GOD

For he that wavereth is like a wave of the sea driven with the wind and tossed...

James 1:6-7

Let us stop the wavering. You have to learn to stick with the Word of God. You must put on the mind of Jesus Christ. Remember, He will direct your path. You have to listen to what He is saying to you. If there is anything that is causing you to go back and forth, then you need to take the back seat and let God take the front seat. Some of you may find yourself going back and forth too often. It is not uncommon to go backward, but there are way too many of us who have the wave mentality. We need to get some stability in our lives.

When you say that you are not going to do something, then do not do it. Stop the wavering. If you say that you are going somewhere, then make sure you go. Do not waver. If you feel strongly that you need to release certain people out of your circle, then go ahead and release them. Don't continue wrestling with it in your mind. The Word of God has clearly said that a "Double minded man is unstable in all his ways."

JANUARY 7

MAXIMIZE YOUR FAITH

For therein is the righteousness of God revealed from faith to faith: as it is written, the just shall love by faith.

Romans 1:17

You might be operating with a little faith or no faith at all. It is time to maximize your faith today. If you do not have any faith, let God fill your cup with it. God told us in His Word that if we have faith of a mustard seed we can move mountains (Matthew 17:20).

If you can just imagine the size of a mustard seed, you will have a better understanding that there is so much that can be done with just a little faith. Now how much more we can do with having a lot of faith. Somebody needs to know today that God is moved by our faith. So, you need to show the Maker that you have faith that He is going to work it out for you. Trust Him with the fullness of your whole heart.

JANUARY 8

NEW BEGINNINGS, ACCEPT IT

Behold, I will do a new thing: now it shall spring forth; shall ye not know it?

Isaiah 43:19

This day is a new beginning. You should expect something new to happen in your life. Do not even look back on yesterday. It is gone. You need to focus on what God is doing and saying in your life. There is something positive in the atmosphere. You will bring forth new fruit. God wants to give you a new spirit. He wants to give you a new mind.

There is a new anointing, a new level of joy, a new level of love, a new level of peace, a new level of strength, a new level of praise, a new level of worship...just know that NEWNESS is all around you. Get excited about a new Word that will come forth today.

JANUARY 9

ENCOURAGE YOURSELF IN GOD

David encouraged himself in the Lord his God.

1 Samuel 30:6

You have to learn to encourage yourself sometimes. I have had to encourage myself many times in life. Some of us have become so dependent on the comfort and encouragement of others until we lose belief in ourselves. As long as you have God on your side, you shall find comfort. You will find peace in Him. You will find rest in Him. You should not get so caught up in people—get caught up in God.

If you start feeling low today, encourage yourself in the Lord. Why not? David did. The Bible says, "And David was greatly distressed: for the people spake of stoning him, because the souls of all the people was grieved, every man for his sons and for his daughters: but David encouraged himself in the Lord his God" (1 Samuel 30:6).

JANUARY 10

WAIT IT OUT—BE PATIENT

...the patient in spirit is better than the proud in spirit.

Ecclesiastes 7:8

You don't have to get in a big hurry, just wait it out—be patient. Sometimes you can move so fast and miss the mark and get ahead of your blessing. I experienced several incidents where I felt that I was overlooked for certain things. I had to realize that God is in control of everything. There are times when things are put on hold by God. It might not be your time for a promotion, a raise, to move to a new job, etc. God knows best. He sees what our natural eyes are not able to capture around the curves, over the bumps and hills of life.

I want you to practice patience. If you have a problem with waiting, just ask God to help you. Today, you might want to tell yourself, "I'm going to wait my turn. I know I am next in line." Don't be impatient and get out of line. "...Stand still and see the salvation of our Lord" (Exodus 14:13).

JANUARY 11

REJOICE

But let all those that put their trust in thee rejoice: let them ever shout for joy, because thou defendest them: let them also that love thy name be joyful in thee."

Psalm 5:11

We have so much to rejoice about this day. You woke up in your right mind. That is enough to make you rejoice and say Hallelujah! You need to rejoice in the Lord for the many things He has already done in your life. I personally do not take anything for granted. Things certainly could have been the other way around. He has been so good to me and is truly worthy of everything. I cannot help but to rejoice and give Him praise. I encourage you to do the same.

JANUARY 12

KEEP PRESSING TOWARD THE MARK

I press toward the mark for the prize of the high calling of God in Christ Jesus.

Philippians 3:14

You need to keep pressing toward the mark...you will fulfill your destiny. You must take it one day at a time. You will make if you faint not. Just think about it. You are getting closer to the mark. Forget what is behind you. "Brethren, I count not myself to have apprehended: but this one thing I do, forgetting those things which are behind, and reaching forth unto those things which are before" (Philippians 3:13).

There is so much that God has for you to do. It is time for you to get off Comfort Street; you have been traveling down that road way too long. He wants you to totally focus on where you are going. You can get ready to walk in greatness.

JANUARY 13

SEEK GOD IN THAT SITUATION

And I set my face unto the Lord my God.

Daniel 9:3

If you are feeling low today, just seek God. He is all the help you need and will provide the answers to all of your problems. You do not need to stop seeking Him because things did not go as you plan for them to go. Did you hear that? I said, "The way you plan them..." You need to seek God like never before about that situation you're facing. You need an answer from Him, and you need Him to move speedily. Once you set your mind on Jesus, He will speak when you are least expecting it and He will move while you're in the midst of a bad situation.

You may be sitting at your computer at home or at work right now. Perhaps, you may be doing something else. You may be in a daze because you do not what to do, or which way to go. To be perfectly honest, you do not need to turn to the left nor to the right, you need to stand still and look to God in the midst of your situation.

JANUARY 14

LIFE IS IN YOUR TONGUE, WHY DON'T YOU SPEAK IT?

Death and life are in the power of the tongue: and they that love it shall eat the fruit thereof.

Proverbs 18:21

Child of God, you have full control over what you are speaking. You should make sure your words are life. Remember, you have to think about something before you speak it. If those thoughts are going to make you speak negative, then you must immediately cast them down to where they came from—the pits of hell. Therefore, you can only speak life this day and forever more.

Your words should be fruitful and uplifting, not bitter and foul. God does not want us to speak words that will cause harm to someone else. Therefore, be careful not to engage in certain conversations. You might find yourself agreeing and speaking against someone. You do not want to do that. If it is not a word that will encourage your brother or sister, then just seal your lips.

JANUARY 15

WORSHIP LIKE NEVER BEFORE

Give unto the Lord the glory due unto his name: bring an offering, and come before him: worship the Lord in the beauty of holiness.

1Chronicles 16:29

We owe God worship. If you do not do anything else today, you need to worship our Heavenly Father. He truly deserves it. If your flesh does not feel like it, you need to tell your flesh, "just get in line and do not start with me." I am certain you are in need of something, and it is going to depend on your level of worship.

You may be expecting money to come to pay an overdue bill. You may be expecting to hear from a company that you interviewed for a job recently. You may be expecting to get a new promotion. You may be expecting to move into a new home. With all of your expectations, you have just been hit with a whammy. Nothing seems to be going right for you. I just believe that if you worship God like never before, you can "expect the extraordinary" to happen in your life today. This is something that only our Father in heaven can do.

JANUARY 16

BE FRIENDLY

A man that hath friends must shew himself friendly...

Proverbs 18:24

Make up your mind that you are going to start being as friendly as possible. You do not have to walk around with a frown on your face. You do not have to be mean toward people. You should have more of a welcoming spirit. There is nothing wrong with being cordial and polite.

If you are not attracting people in your direction, you probably want to check yourself. Your facial expression could push people in the opposite direction. You do not want that to happen. You can actually miss out on the potential friend that God wants to bring into your life. Let God take control of you so that people can see Him in you. Remember, we children of God should exemplify godly essence every day. If you think about it, Jesus was as friendly as He could be, even toward His enemies.

JANUARY 17

GET READY TO BE BLESSED

And it came to pass after the death of Abraham, that God blessed Isaac.

Genesis 25:11

God not only blessed Isaac, He also blessed Abraham, Jacob, Moses, Ruth, Naomi, and so many others who are mentioned in the Bible. He is the same God, and He wants to bless you, too. There is a song that is so dear to me, and it says, "Get ready for your blessing, get ready for your miracle." You should expect to be blessed today. All you need to do is position yourself to receive from God. Do the God thing. I know you probably want to tell someone off today, but ask God to help you hold your tongue. Do not miss your blessing because that is fairly easy to do.

Believe it or not, we can get in the way of our blessings. We can stop the blessings from flowing. Do you really want that to happen? Ask God to strengthen you so that you will not place your hands in sin today either. This is one of the major hindrances. There may be a blessing for you very near, but sin could immediately hinder you from receiving it.

JANUARY 18

DO THE GOD THING

...for the ways of the Lord are right, and the just shall walk in them.

Hosea 14:9

Doing the right thing is to do the God thing. I am sure you have heard, "What would Jesus do?" We can easily get in the flesh and do the wrong thing, but we want to make sure we do the God thing today. We can start by giving God honor and praise, and thanking Him for newness. Get some Word in you this morning so that you can start and finish your day doing the God thing. You can grab hold of your attitude if it is moving in the wrong direction—before you leave home.

Make sure you get to work on time, and have a pleasant attitude. If you are heading to a meeting, an event, or school, please get there on time, too. Bless someone with a kind word. Pay for someone's lunch. Tell someone you love them. Do the God thing.

JANUARY 19

YOU CAN MAKE IT

Prove all things: hold fast that which is good.

1 Thessalonians 5:21

I want you to say these four words, "I can make it." You may have failed at certain things in your life, but that does not mean that you cannot make it. If there was a time in your life when you slipped and fell, just know this day you can make it. Keep pushing! Keep striving! The Bible says, "Behold, we count them happy which endure" (James 5:11).You have stood through many tough times. You did not break. There is no need to fret over the failures of yesterday. Today, you have another chance.

JANUARY 20

LET THE ANGER GO NOW

Cease from anger, and forsake wrath: fret not thyself in any wise to do evil.

Psalm 37:8

Don't be angry. You must let it go. "If the devil can have your morning; he will definitely steal the rest of your day." You have to tell him to leave and that he has no place in your life. Sure, he wants to stir you up with anger. He knows exactly what button to push, too. But you have to denounce every act of him. Do not succumb to his mess today. Do not let him use you to be mischievous.

You need to find out what is causing you to be so angry. It is probably something simple that can be handled in a matter of minutes. If you are having a problem with someone, just confront the issue. If you went to bed with that person on your mind, that means you have allowed the enemy to stir you up, even while you were sleeping. Rebuke him right now. Like Jesus, you have to tell Satan to "get thee hence {away, behind}" (Read Matthew 4:10).You make sure to keep him under your feet because it is very clear that is where he belongs.

JANUARY 21

BELIEVE IN YOURSELF

You can do all things through Christ which strengths you.

Philippians 4:13

Who will believe in you if you do not believe in yourself? I am certain there is something you have always wanted to do, and you stopped because you were afraid to go further. You listened to those people who did not believe in you. Your mindset changed because of what they said to you, and what you said to yourself. You will never thrive off doubt. From this day forward, you must surround yourself with positive-minded people. Most importantly, you need to think positive.

You can go ahead and start decreeing and declaring that you can do all things through Christ who is the One that gives you the strength to endure and achieve. God created you to do wonderful things. He wants you to believe in Him. If you do that, you can believe in yourself because you know that He is on your side.

JANUARY 22

FORGIVE IMMEDIATELY

But if ye forgive not men their trespasses, neither will your Father forgive your trespasses.

Matthew 6:15

There are so many people who are carrying unforgiveness and malice in their heart. You know if you are one of those people. If someone offends you, make sure you forgive them immediately. As a Christian, you have a responsibility to immediately address the issue so that unforgiveness won't set up camp in your mind and make its' way to your heart.

If you are holding unforgiveness toward anyone, ask God to help you to release the bitterness and anger from your heart and replace it with love and joy. He is so faithful to turn that situation around that you all disagreed about. If you suffered any form of neglect at the hands of that person, go ahead and forgive them. It will make a big difference in your life, my sister and my brother. You do not want to carry this burden any longer. You do not have to continue living in bondage. It is time to break free this day.

JANUARY 23

HAVE A GOOD DAY

Oh taste and see that the Lord is good.

Psalm 34:8

Today, you might have a phone conversation with someone about a bill, a job or some other important matter. The representative might end the phone conversation with, "Have a good day, or a great day!" You might even say those words to someone. All and all, you need to make sure that your day is filled with joy and peace. You cannot let anyone steal your joy. This can turn your day from being good to bad. You can prevent that from happening.

If someone jumps in front of you at the restaurant or in the cafeteria line, just silently say to yourself, "I will have a good day." If someone says something out of the way to you, just silently say to yourself, "I'm not going to let anyone still my joy. "I'm still going to have a good day."

JANUARY 24

MY SISTER, MY BROTHER, I ENCOURAGE YOU

Wherefore comfort yourselves together, and edify one another, even also ye do.

1 Thessalonians 5:11

I want to personally encourage you. I do not know what your situation is, but I am here to tell you that God knows. So, if you are feeling a little weak, just know that God will make you strong. His strength will hold you up. If you have started any kind of new task, whether it was going back to college or starting your own business or something else, I want to encourage you to complete that task that you have started. Even if you feel as though you are not being supported; you continue to move forward with your vision.

You do not have to continue entertaining those people in your family that say negative things about you, those friends that are operating with no faith, and those people who say that you are not going to make it. These people actually do not believe in themselves; they only believe in tearing others down. Words of encouragement do not proceed out of their mouth. Therefore, don't expect to hear encouraging words from them.

JANUARY 25

DON'T FAINT

And let us not be weary in well doing: for in due season we shall reap, if we faint not.

Galatians 6:9

You are going to reap a harvest if you faint not. Your situation might not look too good, but don't have an ounce of worry. You have sown good seeds, so you are going to reap. God knows exactly what He is doing. He will not default on His promises. Sometimes people may let you down, but God will never let you down.

There is a season for everything, and yours could very well be today. One day a dear friend of mine who is prophetess told me that God gave her a Word to share with me that it was my season. The next day, God confirmed that Word of prophecy through my former pastor and his wife. I shared that to say that though our seasons might be different, but one thing's for sure, you will reap in your due season.

JANUARY 26

KEEP HOPING

For we are saved by hope: but hope that is seen is not hope: for what a man seeth, why doth he yet hope for?

Romans 8:24

We should not have to "See it to believe it." We need to keep on hoping for that miracle. It is coming. Let's just continue to wait our turn. God has heard us and He sees us. God is working behind the scene for all of us. We need to make sure we stay in partnership with Him.

You may have said that you hope your child will get on the right track. You hope that your spouse will get in church. You hope that you get that job you have been seeking. You hope that you get the customers for your new business. You hope that you get your finances together. I want to say this: "Let's keep hope alive together as Christians." We shall see the manifestation of God's work at an appointed time.

JANUARY 27

BLESS SOMEONE WITH A SMALL TOKEN OF A SMILE

For God loveth a cheerful giver.

2Corinthians 9:7

Sometimes the smallest token (a smile) can bless someone tremendously. Do you want to be a blessing to someone today? If so, just give someone a smile. You do not have to pay any money to smile. How would you feel if you learned that your smile prevented someone from committing suicide? I am certain that would probably be one of the best feelings ever.

One of your co-workers could be in a major storm in their life, and all they need is for someone to give them a smile. A family member or a friend could be getting ready to have surgery, and all they need is a smile. A husband and wife could be going through a divorce; your smile can help them feel better. Someone may have had death in their family, and they can really use a hug and a smile. Please don't think that you don't matter. You can make a big difference in someone's life through Christ Jesus. We need to seek God's face to see how we can be a blessing in the smallest way.

JANUARY 28

LAUGH LIKE NEVER BEFORE, IT'S YOUR MEDICINE

There is a time to laugh.

Ecclesiastes 3:4

I heard that laughter is "Medicine for your soul." I believe that is true. I feel so much better when I am laughing. Some people might say that you do not have anything to laugh about. I beg to differ. I will say that you do have something to laugh about. You can enjoy laughing at the devil today because he thought he had you when your child started acting up this morning.

He thought that he had you when your spouse woke up with hell in them early this morning. He thought that he had you when that driver cut in front of you while you were on your way to work. He thought that he had you when your boss started picking on you within an hour of clocking in this morning. He thought that he had you after you realized you had little gas in your vehicle, but you were still determined to press your way to work {or an appointment} anyway. You have a lot to laugh about. Just stop for a moment and tell the devil, "ha, ha, ha, you thought you had me, but you will NOT steal my joy today."

JANUARY 29

IT IS POSSIBLE

All things are possible to him that believeth.

Mark 9:23

Yes, it is possible. "All {everything} things are possible for you." All we have to do is just believe our Lord and Savior. Do not forget that. Whatever you put your mind to this day, know that it is possible. You can go ahead and expect the possible to happen for you today. You are going to pass that final exam. You are going to make some God connections. You are going to receive that unexpected financial seed on this day. It is possible for you to get free from that sin that has been holding you back. Yes, it is possible.

JANUARY 30

GOD WILL FIX YOUR PROBLEMS

In the world ye shall have tribulation: but be of good cheer; I have overcome the world.

John 16:33

Everyone has had problems at some point in their life. The trials and tribulations will come, but do not let them weigh you down. "Be of good cheer" like the Word encourages. You can declare that "The storm is over in your life." You might think that your problems are too big for you, but guess what? They are not too big for God. He wants to carry all of your burdens. He knows exactly how to fix whatever needs to be repaired. Just tell Him to, "Fix it Lord." I can guarantee you He will.

I know this because I have had problems just like you, and He fixed mine. There are other situations (trials) around the corner, but I am overly confident that God's got it. Sometimes He allows things to happen in our lives. But even so, He knows just what to do. I encourage you to not think about your problems today.

JANUARY 31

LOOK TOWARD HEAVEN

My eyes are ever toward the Lord.

Psalm 25:15

Have you ever just lifted your head and looked toward heaven? God knows that you have taken a moment to reach out to Him. God instructed Abraham {then Abram} to look toward heaven in Genesis Chapter 15 verse 5. Abraham was seeking something from God. Today, somebody is saying, "God I need a Word from You. I desire to learn more of You. I have been looking to my left and to my right. I have even found myself looking behind. Lord, I need You."

I want to tell you that you are looking in the right direction—toward heaven. He is able to give you more of what you are seeking, "Double for your trouble," "Double for your loss," and "a double portion of His anointing." God told Abraham "I will multiply thee exceedingly" (Genesis 17:22). And He will do the same for you.

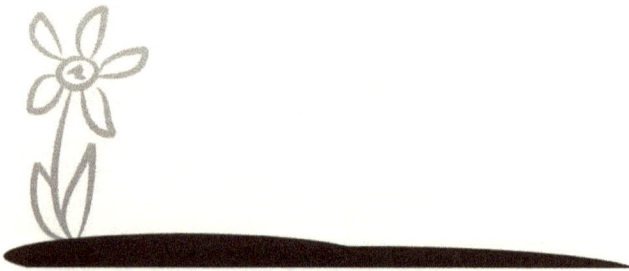

FEBRUARY 1

CAST YOUR CARE ON GOD

Casting all your care upon him: for he careth for you.

1Peter 5:7

All the cares of the world that you have, just cast them on God! When no one else seems to care, just know that God cares. I understand that some things in life can become burdensome, but you must know that you do not have to carry the load by yourself.

Before I learned to depend on God and give all matters to Him, I would try to carry people, their problems, and deal with my situations. Seemingly, I was bound to people. I thought that I could carry all that weight around each day, but I realized that I could no longer carry the pressures of life. I told God that He can have it all. I prayed that He would lift those weights because I had gotten so weak. I began to meditate daily on 1 Peter 5:7. The more I read that scripture, the stronger I got. I give thanks to God, and I encourage you to give Him thanks for He is ready to take on all your cares, too. Just release them—now!

FEBRUARY 2

GIVE GOD PRAISE

His praise shall continually be in my mouth.

Psalm 34:1

Your praise will and can release God's blessings. The windows of heaven will open, and the blessings will shower down. "When the praises go up, the blessings come down." I am certain there are times when you just do not feel like lifting your hands, shouting aloud and jumping up and down, but it is necessary when you want God to release something {wisdom, discernment, anointing...} from heaven.

It is so important to praise God every day. Do not be moved by your emotions and only praise Him after you have received material things and money. You need to praise God for all things, including your health and strength, for being saved, for your family and friends and for your enemies, too.

FEBRUARY 3

CALL ON JESUS

Seek the Lord while he may be found, call ye upon him while he is near.

Isaiah 55:6

If you cannot call on any other name, know that you can call on Jesus. Believe that! Now you do not need to get in the habit of only calling on Jesus when your back is up against the wall—when your rent and car note is past due and you need emergency funds, when you are feeling sick in your body, when you are facing jail time and when you are on the brink of getting fired from your job.

You should call on Jesus all the time. Let's not take Jesus for granted; you cannot use Him. No, it will not happen. You might get away for a short time when you have a tendency to use people, but not with the Creator. So, I challenge you this day to think about the awesome, powerful, magnificent and beautiful name of Jesus. After you think about His name, then I want you to realize that you should call on Jesus not only when things are looking bad, but also when things are going good in your life, too.

FEBRUARY 4

BE JOYFUL

For the joy of the Lord is your strength.

Nehemiah 8:10

Let's get excited right about now! The joy of the Lord is made available to all of us. Yes, that includes you, too. Can you imagine what it would be like if everyone you come in contact with today have joy? Well, I believe that if you can imagine it, then it can happen. Get ready for the experience! The joy that you share will bring about an amazing strength.

This strength will help you to endure the attacks that might come your way today. It will also help you to reject those things that are contrary to God's Word. This awesome strength will also help you to open your mouth and give God all the praise.

FEBRUARY 5

OPEN YOUR HEART

I the Lord search the heart; I try the reins, even to give ever man according to his ways, and according to the fruit of his doings.

Jeremiah 17:10

God wants to do a major cleansing in you. You have to open your heart to Him. He wants to give you your heart's desire, but there is a lot of garbage that needs to go now. You may think that you have it all together, but the mere fact that you have had something against someone for a while, suggests that you need to have an encounter with Jesus. I know I am talking to somebody. Is it you?

Oftentimes we do not think we need help with certain challenges in life. I beg to differ. If we do not get help we can allow certain emotions to contaminate our spirit and our heart. Our Heavenly Father wants us to have a clean heart that is full of love, joy and peace so that we can walk daily with His heart and do godly things. I encourage you to open your heart to Jesus today.

FEBRUARY 6

I AM GLAD

The Lord hath done great things for us; whereof we are glad.

Psalm 126:3

Today, I am so glad. What about you? If you are sad now, just look at someone who is smiling and "happy go lucky" so that you can pull that positive energy into your life. Do not let the cares of this world get the best of you. The negative thoughts that are dominating your mind—I have something better for you to think about, and that is one word—Jesus.

He can turn your day around instantly. Just allow Him to show you how He brought you out of that situation last time. You remember when He came to fix it right on time. I want even go any further...you know all the things He has done for you, so go ahead and cheer up and be glad for the rest of the day.

FEBRUARY 7

GIVE SOMEONE A HUG

Give and it shall be given unto you...

Luke 6:38

A seed has often been linked to money, but it is much more than that. Today, we want to be a blessing to someone by giving them a hug. It really makes me feel special when someone hugs me. How do you feel? Do you feel special when someone hugs you? If so, I would like for you to walk up to someone (your child, husband, wife, co-worker, etc.) and give them a hug.

I am certain that lady who is having problems with her child, and that man who cannot seem to please his wife, and that child who is struggling with peer pressure, and that preacher who is steadily been judged by the world, and that first lady who is enduring abuse and shame secretly, and that employee who has been praying for a financial increase, and that CEO who is now facing bankrupt—all need a hug. There are so many others who need a genuine, godly hug, and you have the arms to make it happen today. You can even give them a smile, too.

FEBRUARY 8

MAKE YOUR REQUEST BEFORE GOD

Be careful for nothing: but in everything by prayer and supplication with thanksgiving let your requests be made known unto God.

Philippians 4:6

If you have a request make sure you let it be known unto our Heavenly Father. Whatever your request is, just believe that He will give you the desires of your heart. Many people request material (the worldly possessions) things from God. There is nothing wrong with that, but we need to begin our day by requesting spiritual gifts so that we can uplift the kingdom of God.

Let's take this day to re-shift our focus on God, and the things that we can do to build His kingdom. There are so many lost souls depending on those of us who are godly to help them. With that being said, we need to ensure that we are seeking God's face and requesting that He gives us the right tools (discernment, wisdom, shield of faith, etc.) to help those individuals who may not be where some of us are in our lives.

FEBRUARY 9

GOD SAID IT

And God said, let there be light and there was light.

Genesis 1:3

From the beginning of time, God spoke light into existence. God speaks to us, and He instructs us to carry out certain tasks, to give a "Word" to someone, to feed someone and to do things totally out of the norm. When He says it that is all that needs to be said!

Do not use a lot of energy trying to tell someone what God told you. The majority of the people you tell are not going to believe you. As long as you know that God said it, then that is your assurance that He is going to see to it coming to fruition.

FEBRUARY 10

RELEASE IT

Let not your heart be troubled...

John 14:1

It is your day to declare that you are going to release it. The guilt, shame, anger, bitterness, worrying, hate...whatever is at the root of what you are enduring, you need to release it— NOW. There is no need to hold on to that bad relationship. You do not have to continue holding on to that job that is treating you unfair, go ahead and start looking for another one. God has something better for you. Let go of the unnecessary debt! You need to let that unfruitful friendship go.

It is okay to let those things go that bring unnecessary stress. I have come to a place in my life where I do not mind letting things and people go. I can tell you that it is one of the greatest feelings to have when you release something that occupies a lot of mind space. It makes you want to have a Holy Ghost party by yourself—and you can, too. I want you to say, "I'm releasing it all right now."

FEBRUARY 11

DON'T BE IGNORANT OF SATAN'S DEVICES

Lest Satan should get an advantage of us: for we are not ignorant of his devices.

2 Corinthians 2:11

Whether you know it or not, our adversary knows when we are being ignorant. He takes full advantage of our ignorance. He has many devices that he throws at us daily. We must be vigilant at all times. We have to read the Word of God so that we are fully aware of his devices.

Think about it. If the enemy can use us today (or any other day) to entertain his mess, or execute his schemes, he will gladly do so. Sadly, many of us will yield our vessel for him to use us. But, wait a minute—you do not have to. Just tell him, "Satan, you are a defeated foe." You should not be afraid of your adversary; you have Jesus on the inside of you. What does the Scripture say? "Greater is he that is in you, than he that is in the world" (1John 4:4). You should appreciate that scripture because it helps you to understand that you are not alone.

FEBRUARY 12

STOP JUDGING OTHERS

For with what judgment ye judge, ye shall be judged.

Matthew 7:1

I will be the first to tell you that I used to have a problem with judging people. I learned through the Word of God that I could be judged by the same measures. My desire is not to judge anyone now. I leave it up to God. He is in control. If you have found yourself judging others, you need to stop today. You have no business or place...there is only One who occupies the seat on the panel, and that is God.

Some people think they have valid reasons to judge others, but no one has a reason. We must learn to remove the 'mote' out of our own eye. It can prevent you from seeing the scope of your problems and circumstances. When this happens we tend to zoom in on everybody else's situation and freely judge them. Today, I challenge you to examine yourself and leave the judging to God.

FEBRUARY 13

DON'T BE ASHAMED OF GOD

For whosoever shall be ashamed of me and of my words, of him shall the Son of man be ashamed, when he shall come in his own glory, and in his Father's, and of the holy angels.

Luke 9:26

I have some questions I would like to ask you, "Who woke you up this morning? Who clothed you? Who fed you? Who saved you? Who is providing for you?" I can go on and on asking questions that you can answer openly or silently. Nonetheless, there is only one answer to all of them—Jesus. If you have a different answer, then either you do not know Jesus, or you are ashamed of Him.

I am here to tell you, as an Ambassador of Jesus Christ, I am not ashamed, and you should not be ashamed. There is a scripture you need to read and meditate on throughout the day. "But whosoever deny me before men, him will I also deny before my Father which is in heaven" (Matthew 10:33).

FEBRUARY 14

LORD, TEACH ME HOW TO LOVE UNCONDITIONALLY

Beloved, let us love one another: for love is of God: and every one that loveth is born of God, and knoweth God.

1 John 4:7

Some of us may not know how to love unconditionally. We must remember that God's love does not come with conditions. We should not expect anything in return but the love of God. We do not have to accept anything less than that. We must also remember that love is rewarding, and we should give love.

If you know that it is hard for you to love with the love of God, then ask Him to teach you. I am overly confident that He will because He taught me how to love. You may think that you have a valid reason not to love your enemies and those who have despitefully used you, but you do. God commands that we love each other. As a matter of fact, "LOVE is one of the greatest commandments" (Matthew 22:37-39).

FEBRUARY 15

TO BE CONTINUED

... He which hath begun a good work in you will perform it until the day of Jesus Christ.

Philippians 1:6

You are just like a cake that is in the process of being baked. You can tell by the way a cake tastes that it was made by a master baker. You know the baker must have put the right ingredients in it, and they took their time to bake it. The temperature was set at the correct degrees, and the right cake dish was used to bake it. I am sure they checked it periodically to make sure it was rising to their satisfaction. You see, they are used of baking so they know if it needs to stay in the oven longer.

God, the Maker is in the process of slowly baking you. And He will put the right ingredients (wisdom, love, forgiveness, peace, joy) on the inside of you. He is saying, "This is my product. I am doing a "new thing" in my son and my daughter. I am perfecting them. I am preparing them for a great purpose. They will do greater works..." All you have to do today is yield your vessel. Let God have His way in your life. He is not finished with you yet.

FEBRUARY 16

LORD, HAVE EVERLASTING MERCY ON ME

O give thanks unto the Lord; for he is good: for his mercy endureth forever.

Psalm 136:1

I do not know what I would do or where I would be if it had not been for God's mercy. I want to take the time to thank Him for not only His mercy, but also His love and grace. There were times when many of us knowingly sinned. And it was God's mercy that kept us in spite of our mess. We must be careful not to take His grace and mercy for granted though. Those of us who know the way must start showing others the way of God by letting our light shine. We can start doing this today.

FEBRUARY 17

BLESS THE LORD

Bless the Lord, O my soul. O Lord my God, thou art great...

Psalm 104:1

There is a song that says, "I will bless the Lord at all times; he's good." I can truly say that He is good. If you could just get a peak of His glory today, you would bless Him even more. You have no reason to be ungrateful this morning. You have every reason to bless the Lord.

"Bless the Lord, O my soul: and all that is within in me, bless his holy name. Bless the Lord, O my soul, and forget not all his benefits: Who forgiveth all thine iniquities; who healeth all thy diseases: Who redeemeth thy life from destruction; who crowneth thee with lovingkindness and tender mercies. Who satisfieth thy mouth with good things; so that thy youth is renewed like the eagles" (Psalm 103:1-5).

FEBRUARY 18

SING A SONG UNTO THE LORD

O sing unto the Lord a new song...

Psalm 96:1

If you have a voice to speak, then you need to lift up your voice and sing a song unto the Lord. No, you do not have to be a well-known artist. As long as you have a mouth, you can make a joyful noise. If you cannot come up with your own words, then listen to a song on the radio and sing along with the artist/choir. God has done so many things for the body of Christ, and He deserves every ounce of our praise, worship and tune that is within us.

I can remember growing up and my mother would walk around the house as she would clean up, and I would hear her singing unto the Lord. I would even hear her hum the words of the song at times. She would go from room to room. You may have experienced your mother or grandmother yielding their voices unto the Lord. And you saw how the atmosphere changed. Everybody seemed to be filled with joy and happiness; all the negative energy had ceased. Today, you can do the same thing, too. Just try it, and watch the atmosphere change!

FEBRUARY 19

DON'T FEAR

For I the Lord thy God will hold thy right hand, saying unto thee, Fear not; for I will help thee.

Isaiah 41:13

So many people are walking around in fear. They have a fear of losing things. When the devil tries to remind you of what bills are past due, the doctor's report, how your family is treating you; you can remind him that "He is already defeated."

As a matter of fact, he was defeated a long time ago. He does not control you. He does not reign above God. He will always be a liar. Somebody needs to know that. Going forward, when he tries to fill your heart with fear, you can boldly tell him "I have faith in God. I know what He can do and will do for me. He has yet to fail me."

FEBRUARY 20

USE WISDOM

...For the price of wisdom is above rubies.

Job 28:18

You can only obtain wisdom from God. It is a gift. You cannot purchase wisdom. It comes from above. I realized that when I did not have wisdom I would seemingly make the same mistakes in life. My prayer was that God grant me with wisdom, and He did. If you ask God for wisdom, He will give it to you, too.

You can start using the wisdom of God, even with something as simple as making a decision of responding in a negative manner if someone offends you. Also, if you are going to gossip or engage in any sinful acts as well. I encourage you to apply wisdom to every aspect of your life.

FEBRUARY 21

GO ON AND PERSERVERE

Thou therefore endure hardness, as a good soldier of Jesus Christ.

2 Timothy 2:3

Some people might ask, "How is she able to keep a positive attitude in the midst of her trials? What is he smiling for after receiving his pink slip from work? Why are they in a good mood when their family is facing foreclosure? Oh boy, "Nothing seems to shake them."

Are you that person who is going through a number of things, yet you are not shaken? Although people might say, "You're crazy; I don't know if I can take it." Well, I say, "It seems like you know how to persevere." The Bible did not say we would not face some challenges in life. However, it does say that we will be persecuted. "Blessed are they which are persecuted for righteousness' sake: for theirs is the kingdom of heaven" (Matthew 5:10). I encourage you to keep persevering, even when you are being persecuted.

FEBRUARY 22

YOU ARE STANDING ON GOD'S STRENGTH

The Lord is my strength and my shield; my heart trusted in him...

Psalm 28:7

I have heard people say, "You just don't know how strong you are." I agree with that statement. If the devil's fiery darts have been thrown in your direction and you are "still standing," then you are definitely strong, seriously.

You may have been on the battlefield for quite some time. You have been in a serious warfare. The devil tried to shake you. He tried to break you. He tried to take your mind. He tried to kill you. But, you are "still standing." Some people might say, "They should have been dead." Today, you can boldly say, "My strength is in the Lord. His grace and mercy is sufficient. He kept me when I couldn't keep myself. Don't you know I am child of the Most High God? He was in the battle fighting for me all along."

FEBRUARY 23

DON'T JUSTIFY YOUR SIN, JUST REPENT

...But now commandeth all men everywhere to repent.

Acts 17:30

We all have sinned, and there are times when we fall short of God's glory. Sometimes we unknowingly sin, and there are other times we knowingly sin. We need to be more cognizant of our behavior and actions. Many of us know right from wrong, especially those of us who are grounded in the Word of God.

If you think about doing wrong, then you have sinned. There is no need to justify, just immediately repent to God for the thought. Remember, every act that is carried out starts in your mind. If you can latch on to the truth of that statement, I believe that you can easily cast down those ungodly thoughts that come to your mind. The Bible says, "Cast down every high thing that exalteth itself against the knowledge of God" (2Corinthians 10:5).

FEBRUARY 24

GOD IS YOUR SECURITY

No weapon that is formed against thee shall prosper...

Isaiah 54:17

"I need a weapon for protection." "I need my husband to protect me." "I need my wife to protect me." You may have used one of these statements, or some other statement. It is not okay to put your trust and confidence in any other form of protection, but Almighty God. He is the strongest weapon any of us can have daily.

People are going to rise up against you. They're going to talk about you, and circumstances are going to overwhelm you. You will come under attacks. You will be persecuted, too. But through it all, God is your shield of protection. The only weapon you need is His Word. You can lean and depend on Him no matter what. He is not going to turn His back on you. So, let Him fight your battle.

FEBRUARY 25

YOU CAN TURN BITTERNESS INTO JOY

The heart knoweth his own bitterness...

Proverbs 14:10

If someone treats you unfairly or make you mad today, do not let it turn into bitterness. You should address the issue in a positive manner so that it will not escalate. Oftentimes small matters turn into big problems because of lack of communication. It can all be avoided, and you can go on and enjoy your day.

If you do not address the problem, you will probably think about it all day. As a result, bitterness can and will make its way to your heart. When this happens, your anger and frustration will usually be taken out on someone innocent. You do not want this to happen. Today, I encourage you to start making the turn to the road of joy.

FEBRUARY 26

JESUS IS THE ONE

Jesus said that I am the way, the truth, and the life...

John 14:6

I can tell you that having a relationship with Jesus is the best relationship you will ever experience. None of us can make it without Jesus Christ. If you feel a void in your life, I can assure that God will be the best One to fill that gap.

He will not mistreat you. He will not talk about you. He will take care of you. He will comfort you. He will sustain you. He will teach you. He will protect you. He will save you from going down the dark path of life. He is our Lord, forever.

FEBRUARY 27

THE ANSWER ISGOD'S WORD

In the beginning was the Word, and the Word was with God, and the Word was God.

John 1:1

The answer is always the Word of God. If you did not know that, you will soon find that His Word provides the best solution to all of your problems. If you are now dealing with something (fear, struggles, bitterness, etc.), just go to the concordance and you will find a scripture that can help you make it through those tough times. You can also purchase an additional concordance that provides more scriptures.

We are in a season that demands us believers to study the Word of God more than ever, and I encourage you to do so. There is a Word for you in the sixty-six books of the Holy Bible.

FEBRUARY 28

TRUST GOD UNLIMITED

Commit thy way unto the Lord; trust also in him; and he shall bring it to pass.

Psalm 37:5

Child of God, do not put limits on God. Tell the Lord, "I am going to trust you unlimited." When you do this, you simply believe Him for everything He will and can do in your life. He does not want you to put full confidence and trust in anyone but Him.

You may have experienced a time that you thought you could trust people, especially someone close to you. But something happened and you were compelled to move in a different direction. You had to turn to someone else, maybe even a stranger. You learned that you could not depend on them. God was in the background all along saying, "Look up, I want let you down. Why want you trust me?" Child of God, it is time for us to trust our Heavenly Father, and you can start today.

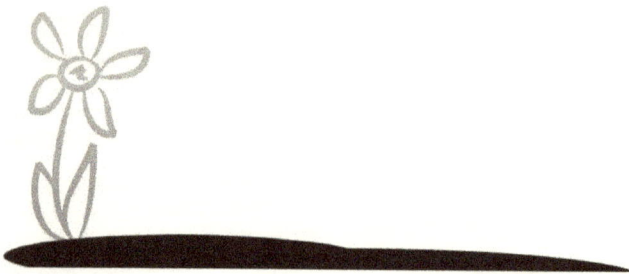

MARCH 1

OH LORD, HELP ME!

Help me, O Lord my God: O save me according to thy mercy.

Psalm 109:26

Some people will say, "Oh Lord, help me," when they are on what we say, "Sick or death bed." You should not want to wait until then to ask Jesus for help. Now, He is honored when you call upon His name, but I know that I personally need Him daily. I need His presence through the good and bad times, sick or well.

God is stretching out His hands to you, my sister and my brother. He wants to help you make it through that hostile work environment. He wants to show you something different. He wants to heal your sick body. He wants to fight that battle you are in. He wants to help you with every matter in your life.

MARCH 2

PRAISE YOUR WAY OUT

I will greatly praise the Lord with my mouth; I will praise him among the multitude.

Psalm 109:30

Do you ever recall praising your way out of any situation? You may need to just "praise your way out" of that dead situation you are currently in. You can combine your faith, prayer and praise, and then sit back and watch God move. Your praise will prevent you from thinking about what happened to you. You will not worry about what people are saying about you, or who is watching you. You have to learn how to praise God in spite of everything.

I remember when I was attending a church service, and I heard the pastor say, "You don't need to focus on the people around you, just give God a sacrificial praise." He said, "You've got to be radical because you need a break through right away." You needed to hear that today!

MARCH 3

WHAT ARE YOU THIKING ABOUT?
THINK POSITIVE

...whatsoever things are true, whatsoever things are honest,
whatsoever things are pure, whatsoever things are lovely,
whatsoever things are of good report; if there by virtue, and if there
by any praise, think on these things.

Philippians 4:8

You need to start thinking positive. Do not continue being a negative thinker. I used to be a pessimistic person, but now I am optimistic. I expect and look for great things to happen in my life, and in my family and friends life, too.

The moment you think things are going to be negative, the manifestation of those thoughts will be negative. We have to be very careful how we think. I admit, sometimes it can be a struggle when things are crumbling around you, but that is when you have to read the Word of God more and more, and surround yourself with positive-minded people. And that includes on your job, in your home, at church and wherever else you find yourself spending an extensive amount of your time.

MARCH 4

MAKE YOUR PLANS BY GOD'S AGENDA

For I know the thoughts that I think toward you saith the Lord...

Jeremiah 29:11

Many of us have our own agendas, and it is acceptable if God is incorporated in our daily plans. If you have not ever asked Him for directions, it is your day to shift gears. You need to start making plans by His agenda. Trust me; this is the absolute best way. He knows what is best for each of us. We need to start asking God for daily instructions.

You might want to say, "Lord, I desire to give you honor today, so what would you like for me to do so that you can be glorified?"He will show you exactly what He wants you to do. He will even tell you what to say. "The best is yet to come" in your life when you follow God's lead."

MARCH 5

YOU ARE VALUABLE TO GOD

...God saw everything that he made, and behold, it was very good {valuable}...

Genesis 1:31

At the beginning of time God created heaven and earth. Shortly after, He created mankind. Each of us is His creation, and we were all made in His image. This day, you need to understand that you are important and valuable to God. If no one else seems to value you, always know that God does.

I have dated men who did not value me. I have worked for companies that did not value me. I have had other encounters where I did not feel that I was valued at all. I have learned over the years that people will take you for granted. Your kindness and sincerity is often used to other people's advantage. God wants to remind you today that you are a valuable human being, and do not let anyone tell you differently or treat you like you are nothing.

MARCH 6

GOD'S OMNIPRESENCE IS WITH YOU

...I will never leave thee, or forsake thee.

Hebrews 13:5

You can rest assure that God is with you. He lives on the inside of you. Today, you need to know this. I want to share a story with you so that you can see that He will always be there with you. One day I was traveling to work and my car cut off. The rear end of the car was still in the road when I drove on the curb. Mind you, cars were still traveling in this lane. I started praying that no one would hit the car while I was sitting in it. Seemingly when I was ready to exit, more cars would come around the curve.

By the grace of God, I was able to get out of the car safely. I started walking toward the gas station that was about three blocks ahead of me when a woman (a stranger that I believe was sent by God) offered to give me a ride to the gas station. I said, "Thank you, God." His grace and mercy was all around me. I hope this story will help you to understand that you might have an obstacle today, but you need to know that God is already on the scene.

MARCH 7

GOD IS PROOF

Prove what is acceptable unto the Lord.

Ephesians 5:10

You do not have to prove anything to anyone. God is all the proof you need in your life. Ask yourself, "Who am I trying to prove myself too?"and "What am I trying to prove?" You must understand that some people are not going to like you; they are not going to support you; and they are not going to respect you. You know what? That is not your problem. You do not need to be concerned with anyone else's thoughts, nor do you need to prove your position to them.

God is the only One you need to prove yourself to by consistently doing what is right and acceptable in His sight. You and God have a personal thing going on. The both of you talk to each other about everything, and you recognize that He is your source. So, let Him serve as your proof today!

MARCH 8

STOP BEING SELFISH

Give and it shall be given unto you: good measure, pressed down, and shaken together, and running over shall men give unto your bosom..."

Luke 6:38

It is a good day to start thinking about others. Lay aside doing something for yourself today and do for someone else. You will feel good afterwards. Having the heart of Jesus will prompt you to always do for others, because "It is not about you."

You might want to ask yourself, "What does it profit me to be selfish?" That might be a strong question, but try answering it. If you know that you are a selfish person, you should ask God to soften your heart so that you can start reaching out to others today.

MARCH 9

WALK IN HUMILITY

Humble yourselves therefore under the mighty hand of God, that he may exalt you in due time.

1Peter 5:6

I believe that God is pleased when we humble ourselves. I like being in a place of humility. What about you? I believe that if you start walking in humility, you will reap God's blessings. If you are walking in pride, putting all your trust in people, looking down on your neighbors, believing that your money and material possessions make you—come down off your "high horse!" There is only One who is at the right hand of the throne of God—and that is Jesus. And He told us that we should "Humble ourselves before the Lord." I encourage you to humble yourself today.

MARCH 10

COMPLAINING IS NO HELP TO YOU

And when the people complained, it displeased the Lord...

Numbers 11:1

It is a good day. Do not complain. If you take a look around you, you will find that you have no reason at all to complain. You have a job today, but somebody cannot work because of their illness. You have a roof over your head, but somebody is sleeping in their car. You have a car to drive, but somebody is walking miles to get to their destination. You have food to eat, but somebody wish they had a piece of bread. You have money to put gas in your vehicle, but somebody is struggling to make it to next payday. You need to know that God is not moved by your complaints. Your faith will only move Him.

All you have to do today is just meet someone who is facing a number of things, but still have a smile on their face. I believe that you can draw strength from them. By being in the presence of people like this, you can also have a greater appreciation for what you already have.

MARCH 11

DON'T COMPROMISE YOUR VALUES

And be not conformed to this world: but be ye transformed by the renewing of your mind, that ye may prove what is good, and acceptable and perfect will of God.

Romans 12:2

God has brought you out of your mess. He has cleaned you up, and "Placed your feet on solid ground." That is right! You should no longer compromise any of your values. You do not have to bow down to anyone but the Great I AM.

There was a time that you probably settled for less; you did not set godly standards, but God has shown you that you are worthy of His best. Now you can tell the devil you are not going to compromise your values—Period. You are not going to buy into his lies and schemes.

Because of where you are in your life, I encourage you to start telling others who are compromising their values that they do not have to continue operating with worldly standards, and that God wants them to raise the bar and operate with His standards.

MARCH 12

FILL MY CUP, LORD

Blessed are they which hunger and thirst after righteousness: for they shall be filled.

John 4:14

Years ago, I would repeatedly listen to the song, "Fill My Cup, Lord." I still love that song; it means so much to me. I want my cup to be filled with the things of God. Can I get a witness? I believe that God wants to give you more than enough today. As a matter a fact, His Word alone is "more than enough."

You are in a season of overflow. Your cup will run over with understanding, wisdom, joy, peace, happiness, and all the things of God. I declare and decree that your family will start coming together. Your finances are about to turn around. Your body is in the processed of being healed. Your spiritual gifts (and talents) will make room for you. Your purpose is about to be revealed. It's not just a matter of time; it is simply your time. The blessings are getting ready to shower down on the people of God. So, I say to you, get ready to receive!

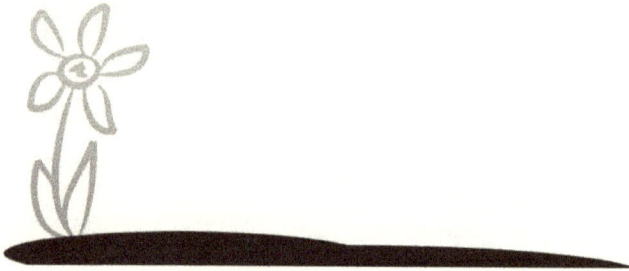

MARCH 13

YOU SHALL

He shall glorify me...

John 16:14

The word SHALL is mentioned many times in the Bible. When it was spoken of in the Bible it was said with authority—by Jesus. God is saying to you today, "You shall inherit the earth. You shall be blessed. You shall see Him. You shall be called the children of God. You shall rejoice. You shall have peace. You shall not be moved. You shall love your enemies. You shall prosper. You shall walk in victory. You shall fulfill your purpose." Today, you shall...

MARCH 14

TAKE MY HAND AND LEAD ME GOD

Nevertheless I am continually with thee: thou hast holden me by my right hand.

Psalm 73:23

We Christians need God to lead us every day through every occurrence. I want to tell you that God sees us as His sweet, little children. He is reaching for your hand today. Let Him hold it tightly. He is not going to harm you. He just wants you to follow His lead. You are trying to run in a different direction, my sister and my brother. You don't have to resist Him. It's time to surrender. I encourage you to grab hold of His hand, and I guarantee that you will be happy with His leading.

MARCH 15

HIS BURDEN IS EASY

For my yoke is easy, and my burden is light.

Matthew 11:30

It is great to know that God's yoke is easy, and His burden is light. That means God will not put more on you than you can truly bear (carry). I have put all my cares into His hands, and I now realize that I don't have to carry everybody else's baggage (problems). Somebody needs to know that there is no need to inherit anyone's problems when you have given yours to God—by faith.

Some people have a made a conscience decision to let go of Jesus' hand. They think that they can make it on their own. When they come to a hard place in their life, instead of them repenting and asking God to forgive them for having a "proud look," they try to throw their problems off on other people. They do not trust God, which is why they let go of His hand initially. Do you know anyone like that? I am here to encourage you to "Let go and let God." You have done all that you can do to help that person. It is too much for you to handle.

MARCH 16

OBDEDIENCE LEADS TO THE GOODNESS OF GOD

If ye be willing and obedient, ye shall eat the good of the land.

Isaiah 1:19

Obedience is totally a requirement to enjoy life—one that is full of promises and fulfillment. We will pay the price if we disobey God. I want to eat the good of the land. What about you? Well, you can start eating the good of the land. You may not have another day to get in order (in right standing) with God.

You can make the choice to obey Him. It really does not have to be a hard choice. It can be easy if you just take heed to God's instructions, and apply His Word to your life. I can assure you that if you continue studying His Word on a daily basis, you will follow His lead and walk in obedience.

MARCH 17

CONVERSATE WITH GOD

Only let your conversation be as it becometh the gospel of Christ...

Philippians 1:27

You can start your day off with having a nice conversation with God through prayer and if possible, steal away and keep the communication going throughout the rest of the day. You need to speak, listen, and then wait for God to speak. Be steadfast. He will give you the answer that you have been praying for.

Holding a conversation with God is similar to holding a conversation with a family member, a friend, a coworker, or anyone else. It is a two way communication. There is no need to be all fancy when you talk to God. He understands each of us and communicates back to us. He clearly understands that some of us are just learning of Him. But we all can contact Him on the same prayer line. That is amazing!

MARCH 18

THAT'S OKAY, YOU'LL BOUNCE BACK

In the world you should have tribulation...

John 16:33

You may have recently lost all of your assets, but at least you still have a sound mind. You can regain what you lost if you just give it some time. You may have recently gone through a divorce, but you are still strong. Maybe you just lost your job, but your needs are still being met. There is nothing that you cannot handle when you have God with you. Therefore, you will bounce back from whatever you recently encountered. I encourage you to prepare for what God is about to do now in your life.

MARCH 19

I NEED A WORD

...Man shall not live by bread alone, but by every word that proceedeth out of the mouth of God."

Matthew 4:4

One day I was driving my car to my son's school and decided to listen to the radio. As soon as I tuned in, I heard a pastor preaching about pressing your way in the midst of your trials and tribulations. He said, "When you have been purposed for something, all kinds of things are going to come your way, but you just keep pressing on." I appreciated that due season Word. Although the enemy tried to bombard my mind with thoughts of failure, I was able to speak the Word of God to him. The devil had no choice but to flee from me.

I have come to know that I always need to hear a Word. I want you to know that God has a Word for you today, and I encourage you to listen for your "due season" Word. God might speak to you through a similar form—through the airwaves. He could possibly use someone on your job to speak a Word to you. He could even use someone at the gas station, or even the grocery store. You just make sure you always keep your heart and ears open.

MARCH 20

CUT THE PRIDE, IT IS NOT GOOD FOR YOU

God hates a proud look.

Proverbs 6:17

There comes a big fall with pride. Be careful not to wear pride. I have come in contact with people who have a whole lot of pride. They will not admit they are wrong about anything. They would rather walk around with their head up high as if they have it all together. If this is you, then you need to cut the pride—today.

This thing called pride has caused many people to fall into a pit that only God can pull them out of. It is quite sad that a lot of us today are full of pride. You do not have to be that way people of God. Look at what the Word of God says about pride: "A man's pride shall bring him low: but honour shall uphold the humble in spirit" (Proverbs 29:23).

MARCH 21

GOD WILL WIPE YOUR TEARS

Weeping may endure for a night, but joy cometh in the morning.

Psalm 30:5

Have you ever been in a situation that pressed down on your spirit and you found yourself crying throughout the night? You prayed, and then you cried more. God knows that you are going to shed tears at times. But He wants you to ultimately depend on Him. He will wipe your tears away forever. Interestingly, when those tears dry, you will have joy again..."unspeakable joy." Today, I encourage you to prepare for a renewed spirit.

MARCH 22

DECLARE THAT YOU ARE HEALED

Who his own self bare our sins in his own body on the tree that we, being dead to sins, should live unto righteousness: by whose stripes ye were healed.

1 Peter 2:24

You are mentally, emotionally, spiritually, and physically healed. If you have been vexed with unclean spirits—you are healed. If you have been attacked with a disease in your body—you are healed. God bore all of our sickness and diseases. "He was wounded for our transgressions. He was bruised for our iniquities and with His stripes we're healed" (Isaiah 53:5).

The headache that you have now, just declare that you are healed. The pain you feel in your back, just decree that you are healed. Just began to lay your hand on whatever part of your body that is hurting and say, "I'm healed in the name of Jesus."

MARCH 23

A RIGHT ON TIME BLESSING

...shall receive the blessing from the Lord.

Psalm 24:5

How many of you would like to receive the blessing that you have been hoping and praying for? Well, this is your day. There is a blessing in the atmosphere, and "It has your name on it." Can you smell it? Can you sense it? Are you ready for it?

You have prayed that God takes care of that unexpected issue. You have asked God to meet some other need as well, and He is. "He might not come when you want Him to, but He is always on time." I decree that your "right on time blessing" will come while you are praising Him today, so you can start reaching up and pull your blessing toward you. It belongs to you. Go ahead and reach wherever you are now! I read in His Word, "when the praising God up, the blessings come down." I guarantee you that He won't default on His promises.

MARCH 24

REAP A GOOD HARVEST

...He that soweth bountifully shall real also bountifully.

2 Corinthians 9:6

The Word says, "In due season we shall reap." That is good news! God remembers every good seed that you have sown. He knows that you have sown bountifully, too. He saw when you gave someone gas money to get to work, when you paid for somebody's lunch, when you prayed for that sister or brother who requested prayer.

He also remembers the kindness and unconditional love you exemplified through those very acts. You have sown a lot of good seeds, so you can get ready to receive a good reward from Heaven. You have very much pleased God with your giving. I encourage you to continue giving because "the more you give, the more you will receive."

MARCH 25

SHHH...BRIDLE YOUR TONGUE

But the tongue can no man tame; it is unruly evil, full of deadly poison.

James 3:8

Some of us may find that we talk a bit much. With that being said, we may lend our ears to conversations that are not pleasing to God. If this is you, I want you to know that it is not okay to engage in every conversation that is going on; however, it is okay to remain silent and just be that light in the midst.

Because some of us talk a lot, we feel as though we need to voice our opinions amid every conversation. You can ask God this morning to help you to tame your tongue. You do not have to be included in the mess today. I encourage you to leave the gossip right where it is. As a matter of fact, when the gossip session starts, just tune it out.

MARCH 26

DON'T BURN ANY BRIDGES

Therefore all things whatsoever ye would that men should do to you, do ye even so to them...

Matthew 7:12

I once heard a wise person say, "Don't burn the bridge that carried you across." That is profound. We all should close our eyes and just visualize going across a bridge to get to an important appointment. This bridge is the only way to get to our destination and the only way to get back from where we came. Now, how would any of us feel if the bridge was torn down by the time we left our appointment? It's sad just thinking about it, right?

I have always related this statement to people and how they treat each other. With that being said, I'd like to say that many of us have burned many bridges. We must be very careful how we treat people, and always remember where we come from. I encourage you to start treating people with kindness, love, appreciation, and respect. Don't burn any more bridges because you never know which one will be your last one.

MARCH 27

GOD CAN REPAIR YOU

...Put on the new man, which after God is created in righteousness and true holiness.

Ephesians 4:24

Do you need to be repaired? Do you need a new heart? Do you need a new mind? Today, you need to seek the best repairer, and that is Jesus. If you think that you cannot be repaired, then I can assure you in the name of Jesus you can. If you have heard people say, "There is no hope for him or her; they are beyond repair." I beg to differ. I am a living testimony. God made me new. He is the same God that will make you a new person, and the process has begun.

MARCH 28

DON'T WORRY

Be of good cheer...

Matthew 14:27

It would be great if you can let this day be a 'worry-free' one. I want to encourage you to trust God. He always makes a way for His children. "Take no thought, saying, what shall we eat? What shall we drink? Or wherewithal shall we be clothed? For you heavenly Father knoweth that ye have need of all these things. But seek ye first the kingdom of God, and his righteousness; and all these things shall be added unto you" (Matthew 6:31-33).

I used to worry about a lot of things, and worrying seemed not to have changed a thing in my life for the better. And, worrying will not make anything better in your life either. Therefore, I encourage you to release worrying today. God is going to take care of that matter that you are overly concerned about. Just trust Him!

MARCH 29

STAY IN THE SPIRIT

And the spirit of the Lord shall rest upon him, the spirit of wisdom and understanding...

Isaiah 11:2

It is an awesome experience when we can practice staying in the spirit. I know that it can be a little challenging sometimes to stay in the spirit, but you have to ask God to guide you the more your flesh tries to pull you in its direction. You have to bring it under subjection. You don't need to give into your flesh. Sometimes we can allow ourselves to get out of line. The flesh always wants to take charge, but it is time for your spirit to take charge.

MARCH 30

THE STORM IS OVER

...When the enemy shall come in like a flood, the Spirit of the Lord shall lift up a standard against him.

Isaiah 59:19

The storm is over in your life. I mean, "It's over now." Some people have been swept away by the storms (trials and tribulations) of life, but thank God you are still here. Every now and again, we will come into a storm. And the rain will cause floods. We just need to make sure that we have everything we need to protect ourselves while in the storm. Remember, it is not going to rain forever; the winds are not going to continue blowing; the storms will soon cease. You can believe that with your heart, mind and soul.

MARCH 31

GET AWAY FOR A MOMENT

My presence shall go with thee...

Exodus 33:14

Have you ever felt the need to just get away from around everyone and everything for a moment? It is so important to get away for a moment—from all the noise, confusion and chaos that seem to surround you. There are times when we need that quiet time with God.

You might have a pressing issue that needs the attention of only God right now. You need to bypass everyone else and get in the presence of God today. Let Him fill your spirit with peace; that "peace which passeth all understanding, shall keep your hearts and minds through Christ Jesus" (Philippians 4:7).

APRIL 1

DON'T DIG A DITCH FOR ANYONE

Whoso diggeth a pit shall fall therein....

Proverbs 26:27

How cruel you think it is to try to get your co-worker fired? How sad it is to try to get your sister or brother put out of their home? How mean it is to plot against your neighbor? How dirty it is to air someone's dirty laundry? These acts, among so many other things, are what I would describe as, "ditch digging."

When you dig a ditch {pit} for someone else, you are in essence digging your own ditch. You must be careful that you don't get caught up in trying to dig a ditch for anyone. Always be mindful that you may "fall therein..." I challenge you today to think about whatever the situation is before you respond in a negative manner.

APRIL 2

MAKE GOOD DECISIONS

...Therefore choose life...

Deuteronomy 30:19

Decisions will be there to stare us in the face every day. When you step foot out of your bed this morning, you need to know that you are going to be faced with making a decision. First and foremost, you may say, "Do I want to comb or brush my hair?" "Do I want to go to work or call off?" "Do I want to cook breakfast or eat out?" "Do I want to be happy or sad all day?"

You must remember that God wants us to make good decisions. We all have made bad decision sat some point in life, so let us focus on trying to make good decisions from this day forward. When we make good decisions, we are basically choosing life.

APRIL 3

TELL THE TRUTH

Speak ye every man the truth....

Zechariah 8:16

Lying has become very common in a lot of people's lives. It is not good behavior at all. We must understand that lies are straight from the devil. As a matter of fact, he is at the helm of all lies. From the beginning of time, he was full of lies.

He has tricked so many of us with his lies and has caused many of us to suffer a great measure of pain as a result of us lying. You should practice telling the truth, even if it hurts you to do so. I believe that you will feel refreshed. I am certain that you have heard "The truth will make you free."

APRIL 4

EXCUSES ARE THE ENEMY TO SUCCESS

And they all with one consent began to make excuses...

Matthew 14:18

Child of God, you have to be ready for the success that lies ahead of you. Make sure you eliminate all excuses. Some of you are full of excuses, and if you would examine your life, you will learn that these excuses have kept you stagnated. You must clearly understand that an excuse is a direct attack from the enemy.

He is against everything that any of us do, especially when we are doing it for Almighty God. Starting today, when you think about making an excuse, think about how it can affect you from moving forward in life. Don't ever let any more excuses hinder your progress.

ARPIL 5

GOD, RENEW MY MIND

Let this mind be in you, which was also in Christ Jesus.

Philippians 2:5

When you have a renewed mind you can operate in a godly fashion. If you still have a carnal mind, then you need to ask God daily to renew your mind. And you need to mean it when you ask Him. Sadly, there are a high number of carnal minded Christians. I encourage you to let that mind that was in Christ Jesus also be in you, my sister and my brother. We can never go wrong when we have this type of mindset.

APRIL 6

DON'T BE IDLE

An idle soul shall suffer hunger...

Proverbs 19:15

If you allow yourself to be idle, you may easily attract trouble in your life. This day you can be productive. First and foremost, make God your priority. Remember, He will always direct your daily steps. He may direct you to give someone a ride to work, prepare food for someone, help lift someone who can't lift themselves, etc. If you really think about it, there is so much good you can do in a 24-hour day. I am certain that you have heard, "An idle mind is the devil's workshop." I believe that there is a 100% truth to this statement.

APRIL 7

THE TEST OF LIFE

...Though it be for a season, if need be, ye are in heaviness through manifold temptations.

1 Peter 1:6

A test of life comes in different forms. I have two questions, "Are you ready for your test? Can you pass the test?" Get ready! You will surely be tested—prepared or not. Think about it. When you are living for God, even if you are not, there are going to be test after test. You definitely should not find it strange when Satan tempts you to do wrong.

Don't let him force you to do anything that is contrary to what you know is right. What you have to learn to do is gird yourself up with wisdom, knowledge, and understanding, and read more of the Word of God. This is your weapon to combat any form of temptation. Sometimes God wants to see if you are going to fight back with what He has already given you—His Word.

APRIL 8

HIS GOODNESS IS AWESOME

Surely, goodness and mercy shall follow me all the days of my life.

Psalm 23:6

Do you want to start experiencing the goodness of God? I can assure you that if you haven't already experienced His goodness, you are in for a treat. It is something about the goodness of God. Can you believe that He is good to us when we are not good to ourselves? That's right! His goodness is far beyond what we can imagine. No matter what trial or tribulation come your way, He is still good. I am certain you may have thought that you didn't deserve God's goodness, but you must always remember that God is delighted to share His goodness with all His children.

APRIL 9

YOU HAVE THE ABILITY

But ye shall receive power, after that the Holy Ghost come upon you...

Acts 1:8

The inner strength that you have will enable you to do some wonderful things in life. No matter what you decide to do, your ability counts because you have the will to finish all the tasks that you have started. God has given you the power to do all things through Him. That inner strength will propel you forward. Today, someone needs to know that your work is definitely not in vain. Just keep the courage and always be willing to work a little harder! You may have heard that "Your work will pay off."

APRIL 10

KNOW YOUR SAFEGUARD

...Whoso putted his trust in the Lord shall be safe.

Proverbs 29:25

Do you know Him? Do you trust Him? Do you desire more of Him? Do you love Him? Do you mind praising Him? Do you like worshipping Him? I am talking about Jesus. I want every Christian to know that He is your safeguard, and you can turn to Him today. He is the One who protects us from all harm and danger. He is the One who watches over all of us. He is the One who guides us around the enemy's traps. He is the One who says, "Yes" when everyone else says, "No." He is so powerful. He is our safeguard.

APRIL 11

LET YOUR LIGHT SHINE

...let us walk in the light of the Lord.

Isaiah 2:5

Child of God, you need to always let your light shine. When you do this, ungodly people will be drawn to God through you. They will be able to see "the God in you." If they see that you are about your Father's business {showing love, giving, praying, etc.} they will want to do the same. Don't waste another day doing things that will not please God.

You can start now showing God how much you want to live for Him and how you want His light to shine within you and through you. You wouldn't be able to count how many people will be drawn to Him.

APRIL 12

EXECUTE GODLY CHARACTER

Ye shall know them by their fruit.

Matthew 7:16

Do you want God to develop your character even more? If you answered "Yes," today is your day to get back on track if you have gotten off track. When we represent God, we should execute godly character every day. God is watching you, as well as others.

Make sure you are in His will. It won't cost you anything to treat everyone kind. It was in Jesus' character to treat people with love and respect, in spite of how they treated Him. If you want to do as He did, you definitely have to make sure you are angry-free. This is nowhere near the character of God.

APRIL 13

CHECK YOUR BEHAVIOR

Be of good courage, and let us behave ourselves valiantly for our people...

1 Chronicles 19:13

How have you been acting lately? Would you say that your behavior has been in alignment with God's Word? Some of us have good behavior, and some of us have bad behavior. If you are one of those people whose behavior need to be put in check, go ahead and look in the mirror and speak to that attitude, commanding it to cease. If you ponder for a moment, you will probably agree that a bad attitude is usually what contributes to bad behavior.

APRIL 14

COMMAND THE DEVIL TO FLEE

...Resist the devil, and he will flee from you.

James 4:7

You have to be very aggressive when you are commanding the devil to flee. You can't be timid, shy, or in a relax mode. You have to command him to leave with authority, power and attitude. It is okay to get mad at the devil. If you just think about all the hell he has caused in your and your family's life, you will open up your mouth right now, commanding him to get away from your children, leave your mind, leave your husband, and everything that belongs to you.

You have to let him know that he is not in authority and that you already have the victory. Tell him that he has to flee in the name of Jesus. It is enough power in that name (Jesus) alone to make him flee instantly. You just have to use that power.

APRIL 15

LEAVE IT ALONE

Let not you heart be troubled.

John 14:1

Some things in life you have to leave it alone. Many times we puzzle ourselves about things that are beyond our control. We try to make sense out of things that don't even make any sense. Why is that so? Whatever it is you have been wrestling with, just leave it alone. You should re-shift your focus on something else.

Each of us know what has been troubling us, and if we are honest with ourselves, we would agree that it has been consuming a lot of our time. It has been mind-wrecking. We don't always know why things happen nor do we understand the reasons during the process, but there is a season when it will be made plain to us. I encourage you my sister to let it go. I challenge you my brother to release it. We have to learn to give everything to God.

APRIL 16

LISTEN TO WHAT GOD HAS TO SAY

A wise man will hear, and will increase learning...

Proverbs 1:5

I remember when my high school band director would say, "Listen, you might learn something." Since I have been an adult I now appreciate that statement and realize that it is very important to listen. When you have a listening ear, you will not only hear what others are saying, but most importantly, you will hear what God is saying.

Today, God wants to say something to you. He wants to tell you about the plans He has for you. He wants to tell you to about yourself. He wants to speak to you while you are in that situation. You need to find a quiet place so that you can hear clearly what God is saying to you.

APRIL 17

RECOGNIZE THE TEMPATIONS

Let no man say when he is tempted, I am tempted of God: for God cannot be tempted with evil, neither tempted any man.

James 1:13

We must understand that every day we are going to be tempted, but not by God. The temptations that present themselves to us come directly from our adversary. You should start recognizing the temptations that may come in any form, whether it is food, material things, etc. Think about it. You may be trying to start a fast because you need to hear from God about a certain matter, and you have committed to cutting back on sweets, but your coworker has brought a cake or some other sweet item to work. Watch out! That is not of God.

Secondly, you may be trying to save money, but you have decided to go shopping with a family member, and you see something you'd like to wear—it very tempting, isn't it? Watch out! That is not of God. There are so many other things that can tempt us, so we must very careful not to fall into this trap for it is not of God.

APRIL 18

MEDITATE ON ONE SCRIPTURE

But thou shalt meditate therein day and night...

Joshua 1:8

If you have a favorite scripture, you should meditate on it today. It is perfectly fine if you choose to meditate on another one. The Word of God is comforting, powerful...complete. We can't live without it. There is a scripture for everything that we will ever go through in life. I remember when my nephew passed away, and I could barely function—for at least a week.

The more I thought about the good times we shared, the tears will run down my face. I had to make a choice if I wanted to stay in that place of weariness or gain joy, strength, and peace by meditating on 2 Corinthians 5:8, "...To be absent from the body, and to be present with the Lord. I had to meditate on this scripture, along with other scriptures daily. We have to realize that we need the Word of God, no matter what. It is the Word that helps us get through everything in life.

APRIL 19

I NEED YOU

Be kindly affectionate one to another with brotherly love; in honor preferring one another.

Romans 12:10

Hezekiah Walker sang a song, "I need you. You need me..." This song is so meaningful and powerful. You would have to pay close attention to the words to this song to appreciate it. As you start your day, realize that you are not in this world alone. You need someone, and someone needs you.

If there is a sister or brother that you may have offended and you know that you need to pick up the phone and call them, you need to go ahead and make that call. If there is a co-worker who offended you and you need to ask them to assist you in a new project, forgive them and ask for the help. Don't let arrogance, pride, fear, shame, or anything else hinder you from receiving something that you may need this day. And you can make yourself available to provide something to someone as well.

APRIL 20

DON'T INTERFERE WITH SOMEBODY ELSE'S BUSINESS

But let none of you suffer...as a busybody in other men's matters.

1Peter 4:15

We as Christian find ourselves in other people's business too much. It is a great need for each of us individually to mind our own. You don't ever have to be overly concerned with someone else's matters. You don't have to use unnecessary energy trying to figure out how someone is spending their money, how much time they are spending with God, what is going on in someone's relationship, and the list goes on.

If you tend to your own matters, you will find that you sincerely don't have the time, the energy, and the mind space to focus on what someone else is doing. You can stay in your lane. There is enough for you to do to keep you busy today.

APRIL 21

LORD, I NEED YOUR GRACE AND MERCY

My grace is sufficient for thee.

2 Corinthians 12:9

We all need God's grace and mercy every day. These two are a great combination. Think about it. If God had not allowed his grace and mercy to be with us when we were in our mess, my God, "Where would we be?" You might willfully or unknowingly do something wrong today. And you may have such high hope and confidence that God's grace and mercy will be there with you no matter what you do in life, and you should feel this way.

However, you should not take His grace and mercy for granted. I am certain that you have heard, "If you know better, you should do better." In other words, if you know the Word of God, you have to make sure you live by it.

APRIL 22

WASH ME CLEAN, LORD

Purge me with hyssop, and I shall be clean.

Psalm 51:7

If you need God to wash you clean today, you should say, "Yes Lord, I need it." You don't have to go another day with all manners of evil in your heart. If you have hatred, envy, strife, jealousy, un-forgiveness, bitterness or something else embedded in your heart, you should ask God to wash you clean. Do you know that these things can hold you back? It is not God's desire that you hold all these things on the inside. These things can bring a great measure of harm to you.

APRIL 23

USE ME LORD

Commit thy works unto the Lord, and thy thoughts shall be established.

Proverbs 16:3

You may have a fresh anointing on your life to preach, teach, minister, evangelize, etc. God has placed a Word in your mouth to speak to the lost souls across the globe. In order for Him to use you at full capacity, you must be willing and ready to "Give yourself away so that He can use you." You should want God to use you at all times.

When you yield your heart, mind, body, and soul to God, you are in essence giving yourself away so that God can freely have His way in your life. He wants to use you as He desires, and not the way you desire for Him to use you.

APRIL 24

LOOK AT WHAT GOD HAS DONE FOR YOU

*He brought me up also out of an horrible pit, out of the miry clay,
and set my feet upon a rock, and established my goings.*

Psalm 40:2

God has done so much in each of our lives. I bet you can shout, "Hallelujah" just thinking about what He has already done in your life. He gave you that new home you prayed about. He gave you the car you wanted. He carried you through school when you thought that you were at the brink of failing. He blessed you with a job promotion.

This is just the beginning, you are getting ready to see God move in a might way. He wants to do greater things in your life. It is amazing how He works behind the scene to do some awesome things in our lives. When we least expect, these things will manifest in our lives.

APRIL 25

REMOVE YOURSELF OUT OF THE EQUATION

The highway of the upright is to depart from evil...

Proverbs 16:17

As believers we need to remove ourselves from anything that God is not in the midst of, whether it is on our jobs, in our homes, at church, or at school. It is not uncommon to engage in matters that we should not take part in, but ask God for the strength to remove yourself from out of the equation. It is necessary to walk away from that which is not of Christ. God has something better for you to engage in.

You can pray for and with someone who needs prayer right now. You can feed someone who is hungry right now. You can speak life into someone who needs it right now. There are so many productive things that you can be doing right now.

APRIL 26

RECONCILE

And that he might reconcile both unto God in one body by the cross...

Ephesians 2:16

We can all rejoice in the Lord, knowing that we have been reconciled to Him. When Jesus died on the cross for us, we were able to gain access to our Heavenly Father. His dying on the cross was all about us. This assignment was placed on Him so that we can get in God's presence.

Today can be a starting point for you to reconcile with those who you have issues with. This is a kind act because Jesus lives on the inside of you. And when you operate with His character, then you can't possibly stay mad with someone who has wronged you. If you take a minute to think about this truth: children get mad with each other and they are friends all over again. As children of God, we supposed to do the same thing.

APRIL 27

GET A HOLD OF YOUR ATTITUTE

Let all bitterness, wrath and anger, clamour, and evil speaking, be put away from you.

Ephesians 4:31

When any small thing can make you become a lunatic, then you are in a serious need for an attitude makeover. You can start getting your makeover today. The first thing I would advise you do is to admit that you have a bad attitude. Secondly, become more cognizant of the small things that make you want to snap and try to prevent it. Thirdly, try to relax your mind. Sometimes your mind can move so fast. Lastly, make sure you are "slow to speak." Don't let your tongue get you in any more trouble. And always, locate scriptures in the Holy Book to read that deal with whatever issue you may have.

APRIL 28

DON'T JUST PUT ON HALF THE ARMOUR...PUT ON THE WHOLE ARMOUR OF GOD

Stand therefore, having your loins girt about with truth, and having on the breastplate of righteousness; and your feet shod with the preparation of the gospel of peace...

Ephesians 6:13-18

When a person is not dressed appropriately during the winter months, they can catch the flu or a bad cold. This is a major attack on the human body. As a result they will probably have to be hospitalized. Now, this could easily be prevented if a person wears proper clothing to protect themselves during this time of season. We Christians have to make sure we are wearing our warfare gear year around to protect ourselves from our adversary's attacks.

We are coming up against a lot attacks nowadays, and if we are not dressed appropriately, we can be consumed by these attacks. If you have been caught without your warfare gear, it is time to put them on. Don't ever think that it is too much to wear. And don't be concerned about what people are going to say. You can no longer afford to walk around without wearing all of your warfare gear—the whole armour of God.

APRIL 29

EXPECT SOMETHING FROM GOD

...I will not let thee go, except thou bless me...

Genesis 32: 26

Are you expecting something from God today? It's time for you to call God to His word. He loves when we give it back to Him. And you better believe that He is going to come through for you. Heaven is going to move as long as you trust and hold on to Him.

I have learned to expect to be blessed abundantly in every area of my life every day. The Bible says, "Jacob wrestled with an angel of the Lord all night long. He touched the hollow of the angel's thigh: and the hollow of Jacob's thigh was out of joint, as he wrestled with him. And he said, let me go, for the day breaketh. And Jacob said, I will not let thee go, except thou bless me" (Read Genesis 32:24-26). Does anyone have that level of expectancy that Jacob had? If you do, then you can truly expect to be blessed beyond your imagination.

APRIL 30

KEEP TRAVELING DOWN VICTORY STREET

But thanks be to God, which giveth us victory through our Lord Jesus Christ.

1 Corinthian 15:57

You are in a great place in your life when you are experiencing victory. When you know that you have the victory, you will feel so much comfort and peace. You will know that it was only God that could have brought you out. When God has allowed you to have the victory over one matter in your life, you know that you can have the victory over another.

Don't allow yourself to get entangled with the things of this world that can bind you. Starting today, you should concentrate on staying on the road you are on—Victory Street. You will soon experience total victory.

MAY 1

MAKE SURE YOUR PRIORITIES ARE IN ORDER

Let all things be done decently and in order.

1 Corinthians 14:40

You may have a tendency to put the most important thing at the bottom of your list daily. There has to be some form of order. Remember, God loves order. You may have been doing things out of order for way too long. You may not even say, "Thank you, Lord for waking me this morning" when you get up in the mornings. You just leave your home and head to work, school or wherever else you have to go.

Today, I encourage you to redo your schedule. You must ensure that you have your appointment with God first every morning, thanking Him for waking you. When you put Him first, He will ensure that everything else on your schedule is completed. You won't have to feel any stress or confusion of not having enough time to get everything done. You will find that your day at work will go smoothly, too.

MAY 2

SET GODLY STANDARDS

I the Lord search the heart; I try the reins even to give every man according to his ways, and according to the fruit of his doings.

Jeremiah 17:10

We Christians need to practice setting godly standards. You may already be there and you need to keep those standards, no matter what. However, if you think that it is okay to compromise your standards for something that is outside of God's will, you are going to have to stand firm. And you can start now.

You should never worry about what people are going to say about you being too godly. You should only be concerned about what God thinks of you. I believe that He is well-pleased when any of us believers say, "No I am not going to do that. You are not worth me going to hell."

MAY 3

AVOID ANY STRESS

Thou hast put gladness in my heart.

Psalm 4:7

Child of God, I encourage you to avoid any stress today. You should not let your circumstances, your spouse, your children, and other people add stress to your life. You need to just go in a relax mode. Don't worry about any cares of this world. Just "let go and let God."

If you think about everything that is going on around you, I am certain that some of those things can add unnecessary stress to your life. Stress can cause headaches, chest pains, neck pain, and so many things. I can remember having those symptoms when I was stressed out over some of the things that were happening in my life. As you can see, stress is an enemy to the human body. You may have heard, "stress is a silent killer." I encourage you to get free from stress.

MAY 4

DON'T HAVE STRIFE

Let the words of my mouth, and the meditation of my heart, be acceptable in thy sight...

Psalm 19:14

It is not very easy for a person to set up strife. If some of us hear that someone has said something about us, even if it is untrue, we become angry and began to setup strife in our hearts toward that person. This is not in God's character. He wants us to love and forgive those who trespass us.

So, you don't want to have strife with your boss on your job if he or she reprimands you for breaking a rule. You don't want to have strife with your spouse for something they did that you didn't like. You don't want to have strife with your friend for not letting you borrow money. You don't' want to have strife with your children for telling you that you showed favoritism. How can you have a merry heart when you are holding strife toward a person(s)? The answer is that you simply can't.

MAY 5

STOP SEEKING GLORY FOR YOURSELF

...no flesh should glory in his presence.

1 Corinthians 1:29

You should never get to the point to where you want self-glorification. What you do for people should never be about you. If you are one of those people who are accustomed to saying, "I" {I did this for her, I did that for him} too often in your conversations, then it appears that it is all about you. Obviously, you want to receive full attention for what you have done. When this happens, that means that you are operating in the spirit of self. Anytime you only focus on yourself, you are setting yourself up for a hard fall.

You should start paying more attention to when you are speaking of you all the time and when you "sound a whistle" while doing something for others. If you notice this behavior, you can tell self to get out of the way. You must understand that God is always the driving force when you are able to bless others with what He has blessed you with. You need to make sure that He is the One that is glorified.

MAY 6

SEEK HELP

God is our refuge and strength, a very present help in trouble.

Psalm 46:1

There are times in life when we are going to need help. We may need assistance in finding a place to live, a job, a car, or something else. God wants to lead us to the right places and to the right people. You must never forget that He is the One who ultimately gives you what you need, and He already has a network of people who are in position to bless you in those times of need.

You must trust that He will lead you to these people and that He has already touched the hearts those in the human resource departments, at the car dealerships, at the realty companies, etc. Just know that all your needs are supplied through Christ Jesus!

MAY 7

FOLLOW GOD

...If any man will come after me, let him deny himself, and take up his cross and follow me.

Matthew 16:24

God loves when we "sell out" and follow Him. When we give up everything that is not of Him and just move in the direction He is leading us, I believe that we will experience an immeasurable amount of peace, joy, happiness, etc. There is always going to be a great outcome when we follow Him. God can lead us through giving us leaders to follow. In essence we will still be following God when these leaders are appointed and submitted to Him. These leaders will hear from God and convey what He has shared with them to help nurture His people and steer them in the right direction. So, go ahead and "pick up your cross and follow Him."

MAY 8

YOUR GIFT SHALL MAKE ROOM FOR YOU

"A man's gift maketh room for him, and bringeth him before great men."

Proverbs 18:16

I want to encourage you today to keep being positive and continue using your gifts. The Bible tells us that they (our gifts) will make room for us. Although things may seem as though they are not lining up, you must continue pushing. Your gifts will flourish more in this season of your life.

You can get ready to be connected to the right people who will have confidence in you and who will support the things that God has gifted you with. Whatever your gift is, use it to the best of your ability. Whether it is singing, tap dancing, writing, acting, drawing, or cooking, just give God the glory.

MAY 9

SHOUT...YOU OVERCAME!

And they overcame him by the blood of the Lamb...

Revelation 12:11

There may be something that you have been dealing with for a long time in your life. You have been on the battlefield, tackling that something that you never thought that you would conquer. The devil has been throwing his fiery darts your way; attempting to destroy you. You must remember that you were not in the battle alone—God was with you.

As a matter of fact, God fought the battle for you. You have overcome, so you need to shout like never before. You should give God the highest praise. You should thank Him for giving you the victory. If you are in a battle now, I encourage you to go ahead and shout like you know you've won the battle.

MAY 10

GOD SHOWED ME MY ENEMIES

Depart from me, all ye workers of iniquity; for the Lord hath heard the voice of my weeping.

Psalms 6:8

You ought to consider it a blessing when God shows you who are working against you. We all know that we share the same common enemy named the devil. However, we must understand that he has those who willfully work with him. In essence, they serve as your enemy. Some of them will come in "sheep clothing."

You have to thank God when He shows you the enemy because you will be able to notice the plots that are being formed against you. Having this insight allows you to get from around these people who are full of jealousy, strife, anger, hatred, bitterness…and they don't mean you any good. Your enemy can be in your home, on your job, in the grocery store, at church, at school, or somewhere else.

MAY 11

I AM WHOLE

Behold, thou art made whole.

John 5:14

If something in your past caused you to be oppressed, depressed, hurt, and full of pain, and you have experienced brokenness, you need to thank God today for allowing you to experience wholeness. We as Christians cannot function properly when we are broken (like a shattered glass). If you are a broken person, how can you be an effective friend, mother, father, sister, brother, spiritual leader, political leader, counselor, etc? It will be very challenging for anyone who is broken to be an effective individual. If you are experiencing wholeness now, please don't ever allow yourself to be broken again.

MAY 12

STAY FOCUSED

...follow that which is good...

1 Thessalonians 5:15

It is amazing how some of us Christians can easily be distracted by the smallest things. This is not good. It also shows the strength of one's focus. If you have been allowing things to distract you, it is important that you not let anything steal your focus. Ask God to help you follow through with your plans and to help you become aware of those things that may try to cause distractions in your life from now on.

MAY 13

I NEED A FRESH ANOINTING

I shall be anointed with fresh oil.

Psalm 92:10

There are some things that we can do that may cause the anointing on our lives to be stripped from us. For example, you may find yourself gossiping about someone and defaming their character when you should be encouraging that person. This is just one act among so many other acts that God does not approve.

When you are working as an ambassador for Christ and wearing the anointing, you must be careful that you don't get caught up in things that will cause the anointing to be taken away from you. If you know that you have been one of those people who have succumb to something that has not pleased God, and have not felt the strength of the anointing on your life, you need to ask God for a fresh anointing. Be careful how you wear the anointing as it is very strong. I am certain that you have heard that it is the "anointing that destroys the yoke."

MAY 14

SOMEBODY'S WATCHING YOU SO HAVE INTEGRITY

Judge me, O Lord; for I have walked in mine integrity: I have trusted also; therefore I shall not slide.

Psalm 26:1

We as Christians are being watched every day. It is almost like people have us under a microscope, and they can see everything we do, and hear every word we say. We are expected to walk, look, and talk just like our Heavenly Father. Therefore, if we are doing something that is contrary to the Word of God, we may have our integrity questioned.

Women and men of God, make up in your mind on today that you are going to try your best to live by what you preach to others. Be mindful that you are being watched on a daily basis.

MAY 15

HE BLESSED ME JUST BECAUSE

For the Lord God blesseth thee, as he promised thee...

Deuteronomy 15:6

Have you ever felt like God blessed you just because? The road may have been a little rocky in your life, but you have still pressed your way to the house of the Lord. You have still trusted God in spite of your situation. Some of you may agree that you didn't deserve the blessings God just poured upon your life. And it had to have been just "because of who you are."

He blessed you just because you sowed that seed in someone's life a year ago. He blessed you just because you forgave your coworker immediately for what they did to you. He blessed you just because you stay focused. He blessed you just because you have been faithful. He blessed you just because you wanted it. He blessed you just because you still loved that person unconditionally who treated you so badly. He blessed you just because He can. You must know that God wants to continue blessing you just because...

MAY 16

DANCE LIKE DAVID DID

And David danced before the Lord with all his might...

2 Samuel 6:14

We owe God a crazy praise, a shout, and we ought to dance like David did according to scripture for what He has done in our lives. Think about it. God doesn't owe us anything. He can do or He cannot do. That is totally up to Him. But, just because He loves us, He blesses us unlimited.

Today, you need to offer God a dance like you have lost your mind. He snatched you from the out of the hands of the enemy. He stopped the foreclosure process. He erased that extensive debt. He blocked the attack on your child. He shut up the mouth of the enemy that has been speaking against you. And He is still working on your behalf to take care of some other matters in your life. He has already loosed the angels to fight for you. You ought to say, "Hallelujah!"

MAY 17

GOD PROVIDES

Therefore I say unto you, take no though for your life, what ye shall eat, or what ye shall drink; not yet for your body, what ye shall put on...

Matthew 6:25

God will forever be in the providing business. He has all the supplies we need from food to clothing to housing to transportation to jobs to everything in between. This is something we never have to question.

I want to encourage someone who doesn't have a job or who may be living with someone else temporarily or who doesn't have a car yet to just hold on, "God has it." In spite of what your current situation is, just know that God is still providing for all your needs as well as your wants.

MAY 18

FOR YOUR GOOD

And we know that all things work together for good to them that love God, to them who are the called according to his purpose.

Romans 8:28

Sometimes God will shift things in our lives. You may be moving in one direction, thinking you are going in the right direction, but suddenly, things may shift in your life. You may experience a number of things that may appear to be bad, but they are good. So, don't become discouraged when God moves something or someone out of your life.

Don't resist what He is doing, child of God. He can see around every corner, and He knows exactly what's ahead of you. We must all trust that whatever God does in each of our lives, it is all for our good.

MAY 19

GIVE GOD YOUR BEST

By faith Abel offered unto God a more excellent sacrifice...

Hebrews 11:4

We children of God don't always give God our best. No matter what some of us do, we will give only partial. If you are a person that is used to giving God partial, you need to be mindful that you have to give God your best. He doesn't want just a partial praise, a partial commitment, a partial offering, a partial hallelujah, and a partial worship...a partial anything.

He wants your best. You should stop making excuses as to why you didn't give your best, just start doing better, so that God will be pleased with what you are giving (offerings, gifts, praise, worship, service, etc.). The Bible tells us that Cain and Abel both brought their offering to God. God respected Abel's offering because He gave his best. (Read Genesis, Chapter 4).

MAY 20

PURSUE GOD

...learn of me; for I am meek and lowly in heart: and ye shall find rest unto your souls.

Matthew 11:29

Oftentimes we pursue everything else but God. We need to really get serious about our walk with God, and we need to start pursuing Him like never before. In order to pursue Him, you need to learn about Him. Once you learn about Him, then you would come to know that He has everything you need. Some of us will find so many things that we believe are important to us and for us, and we will immediately start pursuing it.

If we see someone that we are interested in dating, we immediately start pursuing. If we desire a certain type of job, we will pursue until the position is filled. There are many other things that we will chase. Why is it that we can't pursue God immediately after we learn of Him? This is something that many of us need to think about today.

MAY 21

BE FEARLESS

...fear not, for I am with thee, and will bless thee...

Genesis 26:24

There are a substantial number of children of God who are living in fear. If you have been one of those people, it is time to let it go. God is on your side, so you don't have to fear. You must understand that fear is just the opposite of faith. Remember, the faith that you have will move God. But the devil can smell the fear in you, and he thrives off it. If you fear that you will lose your car, it can happen. If you fear that you are going to lose your job, it can happen. The things you fear can come to fruition if you don't replace it with faith.

MAY 22

DO IT IN EXCELLENCE

Daniel was preferred above the presidents and princes, because an excellent spirit was in him...

Daniel 6:3

Child of God, whatever you do today, make sure you do it in excellence. You should never think that it is okay to have the "I am going to do barely enough; that will get me by" attitude. Don't ever half-do your job. Don't ever half-do your schoolwork. Don't ever half-clean your house. When you half-do things, you will always have shabby results.

You must always remember that others are watching you from the first time you have an encounter. And people can easily detect if you are a person of excellence. When you do things in excellence, you can receive promotions on your job, recognition from others, and favor from God, among many other things.

MAY 23

I NEED FRESH PEACE

Seek peace, and pursue it...

Psalm 34:14

We will always need the peace of God. Some trials and tribulations will come by surprise to decrease our level of peace, and there will be circumstances that may come to steal our peace.

If you have ever experienced an attack on your mind, I am certain you know how it feels to have no peace. I want to let you know today that God wants to give you fresh peace. I am talking about that peace that will calm your fears, replace the pain and hurt that you may be dealing with, the kind of peace that will saturate your mind, etc.

MAY 24

DO SOMETHING SPECIAL FOR YOURSELF

...Whatsoever ye do, do all to the glory of God.

1 Corinthians 10:31

Some of us are always doing things for other people, and we will often neglect ourselves. If you are one of those people, you must learn to do something for yourself; although, it is a kind gesture to do for others. When you kindly do things for others, it shows just how big your heart is. Always remember that you are a special person to God, and He wants you to also do something special for yourself. You can start treating yourself today.

MAY 25

GOD SEES YOUR RIGHTEOUSNESS

For the righteous Lord loveth righteousness.

Psalm 11:7

God knows and sees everything we do, whether it is right or wrong. We as Christian should want to maintain a righteous lifestyle. God is well-pleased when we walk upright. If someone tries to get you to engage in activities that you know within your heart and soul are not right, you should turn and go in a different direction.

I am certain that you have heard, "When you know better, you have to do better." That principle is parallel to what the Bible tells us about choosing life or death. If you choose life, then you have chosen that which is good. Likewise, if you choose death, you have chosen that which is bad. Which one will you choose today?

MAY 26

DON'T BE AFRAID TO LET GO

Turn not to the right hand nor to the left: remove thy foot from evil.

Proverbs 4:27

There will come a time in our lives when we just simply have to let things, people, and places go, and we can't be afraid to do it. As these seasons change in each of our lives, things will change, people will leave out our lives and people will come into our lives.

You must be willing to listen to what God is speaking in order for you to hear what you need to release, who you need to release, and where you should no longer go. Some people, places and things are only in your way to keep you in bondage. Any representation of evil has to be immediately dismissed.

MAY 27

GOD WILL OPEN A NEW DOOR

Knock and it (a new door) shall be opened unto you.

Matthew 7:7

It is a mystery to some of us when certain doors have been closed. But you have to be very optimistic, knowing that God is getting ready to open a new door for you to walk through. You will be amazed when you walk through the door because there will be an overflow of blessings. You may have heard, "When one door closes, another door opens." I want to encourage you today to not be dismayed, distressed or disappointed because a door has been closed in your life. The right door is about to open for you.

MAY 28

GOD WILL EXALT YOU

He shall exalt the...

Psalm 37:34

All you have to do is continue doing the things that pleases God. You will find that he will soon exalt you. He will take you to places you have never been. He will show you things that He hasn't shown others. He will increase you in every area of your life. You don't ever have to be concerned with whether or not people will exalt you for the good things that you have done. God will do the exalting.

MAY 29

DON'T SAID IT, CONTROL YOUR TONGUE

Not *that which goeth into the mouth defileth a man: but that which cometh out of the mouth, this defileth a man.*

Matthew 15:11

We as Christians cannot just say anything we want to say to people. Everything that you say out of your mouth is not acceptable. Although it is common for many of us to say some of the worst things to people when we are upset, it does not mean that it is right. You must learn to control your tongue. You have to try your best to control it at all cost. The scripture clearly tells us that the words that come deep from within us are what defile us. Don't let the words you use defile you today.

MAY 30

THE WORTHY ONE

...but he (Jesus) that cometh after me is mightier than I, whose shoes I am not worthy to bear

Matthew 3:11

God is and will always be the worthy One. He should always be above everything and everyone in our lives. No one will ever deserve the worthiness that Jesus deserves. He went to the cross for us. He loves us in spite of our mess. He forgives us when we don't forgive ourselves and when others don't forgive us.

He holds us close to Him. He comforts us when we are lonely. He gives us a peace of mind. He is patient with us. He perfects our imperfections. He brings clarity to those things that are confusing to us. He does so much for us. He is so worthy. Don't you agree?

MAY 31

YOUR PURPOSE IS AT HAND

...And a time for every purpose under heaven.

Ecclesiastes 3:1

You already know that you have a purpose which is why you have been seeking God about it. I am here to tell you that your purpose is at hand. You need to start walking in it. Rick Warren says, "Passion produces purpose." What is it that you are so passionate about doing? Have you already been doing it? If so, continue to do whatever that something is and you will see it grow more and more. God will guide you in your purpose. He will make the necessary provisions in order for it to be completely fulfilled.

JUNE 1

GOD WILL MAKE IT PLAIN

God shall reveal even this unto you.

Philippians 3:15

You may have been praying a lot about something that you have been wrestling with in your mind. You just want God to make everything plain to you. Guess what? He will do it for all of His children. I recently faced something in my life. I needed to know which way I should go.

I began to pray to God about it, and then I asked Him to make it very plain and break it down to the least common denominator. I didn't want to wrestle with that situation any longer. God answered my prayer. And I know He will answer yours as well. He will make it all plain to you if you believe. He may reveal it to you through a dream. He may reveal it to you through meditation. He may reveal it to you through many forms. Just get ready!

JUNE 2

PREPARE YOURSELF FOR A NEW BREAKTHROUGH

Thy blessing is upon his people.

Psalm 3:8

You better believe that your breakthrough is coming, so you can go ahead and prepare for it. The things that haven't been going right in your life are getting ready to shift. As a matter of fact, they are going to be completely moved out of your way.

You having been praying and hoping for a breakthrough, and God has honored your prayers. The things that you have desired are coming to you. Just start speaking, "money is coming to me now, healing is coming to me now, deliverance is coming to me now, peace is coming to me now, a job is coming to me now. All the things that God has for me is coming to me now."

JUNE 3

IT'S NOT TOO LATE

For God so loved the world, that he gave his only begotten Son, that whosoever believeth in him should not perish, but have everlasting life.

John 3:16

Have you ever scheduled an appointment and if you didn't make it within the time allotted, you had to reschedule because you were too late? I certainly have. I want to share that we have a spiritual appointment everyday with God to get it right. If you are reading this book and have not received Jesus as your Lord and Savior, it is not too late.

He is waiting for you. He doesn't want you to reschedule because as long as you have the breath of life, you have a new opportunity to get it right. You can choose this day. He loves you, and He has given you another chance. He is the "God of a second chance." Don't delay another day. It is time.

JUNE 4

ASK GOD FOR DISCERNMENT

...Sixty score thousand person that cannot discern between their right hand and their left hand.

Jonah 4:11

If you ask God for discernment, I believe that He will grant you with it. He is just that faithful. During these evil times we need a spirit of discernment. We can come up against so many evil activities in a day. I like to think of discernment as having radar. You know a radar determines the direction of an object.

Like a radar, we need the spirit of discernment so that we can detect these evil things that are being formed against us. As we detect these things through the spirit of discernment, we can go into deep prayer, and we can use the power God gave us to combat these things.

JUNE 5

THE ONLY SOURCE

...No man cometh to the Father but by me.

John 14:6

There is no other source—God is our source. Do you believe that? If you will just acknowledge Him and believe in Him, you will learn that whatever it is you need in life, He will graciously place it at your feet. Too often, some people think that their job, their money, and other people are their source. They will glorify these things, and the people they give credit to for the blessings that have been bestowed upon their life. You should never give other people glory; only give God glory because He is your only source. He is such a way maker. He is a door opener. He is the One who all of us can count on all the time.

JUNE 6

GET OUT OF THE DARK

The light of the body is the eye: therefore when thine eye is single, they whole body also is full of light; but when thine eye is evil, thy body also is full of darkness.

Luke 11:34

When we willfully commit sin it blinds us and keeps us in a dark place in our lives. When those dark clouds shadow us we can't clearly see what God is trying to do in our lives. As we turn away from these things that are not like God, the light of God will shine upon us.

If you are a person who is deep in sin now, I encourage you to pray to God for strength so that you can get out of it. Remember, God does not tempt us to sin. He wants us to live holy so that we can draw other people closer to Him.

JUNE 7

TAKE FULL RESONSILBITY FOR YOUR ACTIONS

...I have sinned: for I have transgressed the commandment of the Lord.

1 Samuel 15:24

Many of us love to play the "blame game." We have to come to a place in our lives where we can start taking full responsibility for our actions. If you a person who always blame people for your mistakes and your behavior, you must learn to point the finger at yourself.

There is no need to keep pointing it at other people, saying, "They made me do that; they are the reason I don't have this or that." It is no one else's fault that you are where you are in life. You must start thinking with a sound mind so that you can move in a whole different direction. I encourage you to let God help you get it together starting today.

JUNE 8

SMILE IN THE MIDST OF YOUR TROUBLES

Though I walk in the midst of trouble, thou wilt revive me...

Psalm 138:7

We are all going to have troubles in life. You have to learn how to smile in the midst of your troubles. If you are thinking, "How can I expect to smile in the midst of my troubles?" Well, if you don't put too much energy on the problem at hand, you will find it much easier to smile in spite of what you are going through. You may learn that someone else's troubles are much difficult than yours. Although it may seem hard to smile in the midst of your troubles, just give it a try anyway. A big smile will certainly make you feel better.

JUNE 9

IT'S OKAY, OPPOSITIONS WILL COME

They conspired against him (Joseph) to slay him.

Genesis 37:18

As Christians we will have oppositions that will come. One thing to remember is that opposition will always arise when you are moving forward. When Joseph was trying to move forward and walk out the vision that God showed him, then his brothers served as an opposition. They tried to harm him (Read Genesis—Chapter 37). Don't ever find it strange when oppositions come when you are walking in your purpose. It is almost like the proper procedure as far as our adversary's concern.

It is all designed to get you off track. I encourage you not to give up. It is always okay because opposition will come when you are on the right track in life. Today, you can choose to deal with opposition in a godly fashion or otherwise.

JUNE 10

TRY FASTING

...this kind goeth not out but by prayer and fasting.

Matthew 17:21

As you can see, there are some things in life that we must pray and fast about. I believe that when any of us come to a place where we are confused about something, we need to consider fasting. Don't ever feel like you are too good to fast as the Bible tells us that fasting will basically move some things that don't want to bow down.

Fasting will give you that much needed power to cast out those stubborn demons that don't want to leave your children, you spouse, your boss, your family members, and even some of your church members. Fasting will bring you even closer to God. You will feel more of a spiritual connection with the Father when you fast.

JUNE 11

A MIGHTY GOD

They were all amazed at the mighty power of God...

Luke 9:43

God deserves praise for of all the mighty works that He has done in our lives. He continues to do great things for His children. He never changes, and the mighty things that He has done before in your life, He will do it again. If He healed your body once, He will do it again. If He provided money that you didn't have for that unexpected bill before, He will do it again. If He delivered you from substance abuse before, He will do it again. If He protected you from danger before, He will do it again. Today, I encourage you to continue praising Him for His mighty acts. Don't stop after He does something miraculous in your life; just turn your praise up a notch higher.

JUNE 12

DON'T YIELD TO YOUR FLESH

...The spirit indeed is willing but the flesh is weak.

Matthew 26:41

We are going to yield to our flesh, but we need to try to bring it under subjection when it rises up. Many times we operate out of our flesh. We do things that we shouldn't do, and we say things that we shouldn't say. If you yield to your flesh, you are in essence yielding to your adversary.

You are giving him permission to "have his way" when you should be yielding to the Spirit of God, telling Him to "have His way" in your life. At times, it will be a battle to stay in the spirit, which is why you have to pray daily that you are not tempted by Satan's baits. Moving forward, I encourage you to become more cognizant of when you are in the flesh.

JUNE 13

RECOMMEND JESUS

...A witness of the sufferings of Christ.

1Peter 5:1

I want to encourage you today to recommend Jesus to those who don't know Him. There are a vast number of people who haven't accepted Jesus in their lives because they don't really know Him. It is us Christians responsibility to witness to these people. You have a fresh opportunity to share your experiences with them. Let them know how God heard your cry and answered your prayers. Let them know that what He has done for you, He can and will do it for them, too.

JUNE 14

COMMIT TO CHANGE

Let this mind be in you, which was also in Christ Jesus.

Philippians 2:5

There has to be some form of commitment within each of our hearts to change. Although change is not always an easy thing to do, with God we can become better people. If you are a person who has been struggling with the same old thing, and you want to change your ways, just pray to God about it and make a commitment to do better. You don't have to stay in the same place in your life. You don't have to pay any money to change. A commitment is always great. God sees it all—your stride, your commitment, your dedication and everything else.

JUNE 15

GET TOUGH AND RADICAL FOR THE THINGS OF GOD

I will give unto thee the keys of the kingdom of heaven...

Matthew 16:19

It is time for us Christians to get tough and radical for the things of God. He has given us the keys of the kingdom of heaven. We have to get more serious about helping to build His kingdom, and we shouldn't let anything stop us.

There has to be a strong determination in order for you to be radical in your ministry, in your home, on your job, and everywhere else you go to do God's work. And you can do His work well, even outside of a building. Don't think because you are not at church all the time that you can't do His work; there is a lot to be done in the communities, too. Go ahead and get tough and radical today!

JUNE 16

DOUBLE FOR YOUR SHAME

"For your shame ye shall have double…"

Isaiah 62:2

You may have been talked about like a dog. You may have done some things that you were not pleased with. Something may have happened to you that brought you so much shame. One thing to remember is that our adversary always wants us to feel the guilt and shame of the things that happened to us in our past and the things that some of us are facing now. Don't entertain him because he hates everything about you. He hates what's destined for you.

Today, you can wipe your tears. You can stop thinking about it. You can move away from it. You can release it to the Master. God wants to give you "double for your shame." I encourage you to start giving God thanks every time the enemy tries to remind you of your past. God is bigger than whatever happened to you in your past.

JUNE 17

SEPARATE YOURSELF FROM ANGRY PEOPLE

"Make no friendship with an angry man: and with a furious man thou shalt not go: Lest thou learn his ways, and get a snare to thy soul."

Proverbs 22:24-25

There are times in our lives when we befriend people based on what they look like and what they have. We may notice small things about them that we don't care for, but we try to deal with them. We often pay close attention to their attitude. We can usually detect whether or not they are an angry person from the beginning. Yet many of us will overlook that, too. Well, at least until they become angry with us.

If you know that you are around an angry person, you need to move in another direction. I am certain that you have heard that spirits do gravitate. You have to separate yourself before you become just like them. You don't want to learn any of their ways. Starting today, I encourage you to let God select your friends.

JUNE 18

IMAGINE TOUCHING THE HEM OF JESUS' GARMENT

...And behold, a woman, which was diseased with an issue of blood twelve years, came behind him, and touched the hem of this garment.

Matthew 9:20

The Bible talks about a woman who touch Jesus' garment, and she became healed from the crown of her head to the sole of her feet. She was refreshed and renewed. She no longer had to deal with the pain that she felt as a result of her ailment.

If you are dealing with any issue today, you should just close your eyes and imagine touching the hem of Jesus' garment. He can erase whatever it is you are dealing with—with just one touch. You see, this woman didn't have to repeatedly touch Jesus. It was just "one touch" that pulled the virtue {strength} out of Jesus. He even asked the question, "Who touched me?" He is asking that same question to you right now as you reach out to him. I encourage you to have faith that He will heal your infirmity.

JUNE 19

CONFESS YOUR FAULTS

Confess your faults one to another....

James 5:16

Would you say that you have any faults? If so, you can start off today confessing your faults one after another. When we want to be purified from certain things in our lives, we have to decide whether or not we want to hold on to those things that keep us in bondage.

Remember, none of us on earth are perfect. We are going to make mistakes. We are going to "slip and slide." We are going to do right and wrong. The major key to all of this is to just confess your faults. Repent for your wrong doings. God is the One who will cleanse you from everything. I encourage you to start confessing today, and watch God cleanse you.

JUNE 20

LOVE YOUR ENEMIES, TOO

But I say unto you, Love your enemies...

Matthew 5:44

Oftentimes people can show us love and we have a problem showing them love. Love is the greatest commandment, according to the Bible. We have to learn to give love and not only receive it. Even though our enemies may not show us love, we still have to love them in spite of how they feel about us.

Your enemies could be a number of people from your family members to your friends to a stranger. If you would just focus on loving your enemies like the Word encourages us to do, then you won't have time to be angry toward how your enemies have treated you. God will make your enemies your footstool. You have to believe His Word, even when it seems like your enemies have the upper hand. You have to see them as your footstool even in the midst of them coming against you.

JUNE 21

DON'T QUENCH THE HOLY SPIRIT

Quench not the Spirit.

1 Thessalonians 5:19

Oftentimes we will quench the Holy Spirit. We will ignore what God is saying to us. God placed the Holy Spirit inside of us so that we can have power. Have you ever noticed when you were thinking about doing wrong and something whispered in your ear, "Don't do that." Well, that was the Holy Spirit giving you the opportunity to do right.

When you don't listen when God is speaking, and you make a decision to do what you want to do, you are in essence disobeying God. You need to always be in tune to the Holy Spirit because He is always speaking, and you have to heed to His voice. He is there to help all of us daily.

JUNE 22

I SHALL NOT WANT

The Lord is my shepherd; I shall not want.

Psalm 23:1

Child of God, it is time to realize that God is our shepherd. Everything in this world belongs to Him. There is nothing that any of us can have a need for, and God not supply it. Whatever your heart's desire is today, just take it to the throne room and pray about it. He is ready to meet that need that you and your family, your friends, your neighbors, and others have.

If your heart desires more peace, a car, a spouse, a job, a house, a raise, a spiritual promotion, or anything else, just know that "God's got it!" There is always perfect timing that God will give you the desires of your heart; all you have to do is delight yourself in Him.

JUNE 23

GOD GOT YOU COVERED

...I have covered thee in the shadow of mine hand...

Isaiah 51:16

Child of God, you are covered on every end. There is nothing that is big and bad enough to stand up against Almighty God. Today, if you are feeling like you are all by yourself, one minute you are up and the next minute you are down because the situation you are facing is getting the best of you, I want to encourage you that you are covered by Him. He sees everything that you are facing.

He is your protection when your enemies try to defame your character. He is your mouthpiece when you are not able to speak for yourself. He is your shelter when you need it. He is your judge when people say that you are the culprit. He is your strength when you are feeling weak. He is your healer when you are sick. He is your deliverer when you are in bondage. He is everything you need every day.

JUNE 24

CRAVE PEACE

...Peace be within thee.

Psalm 122:8

There is so much confusion going on around us every day. We must ask God for peace while we are going through the storms of life. When we crave peace just as we have cravings in our flesh, we will obtain it.

There are times when we are going to face things that add stress, worry, pain and hurt to our lives. These things leave our spirits down and troubled. During these trying times, we need the peace of God to help us get through them. Today, you can crave peace. You can have it.

JUNE 25

SEARCH THE SCRIPTURES

Search the scriptures: for in them ye think ye have eternal life: and they are they which testify of me.

John 5:39

There is always a need for us to search the scriptures. While all the scriptures are true, you can search the scriptures that will fit your current situation. God will give you revelation as you read those scriptures based on what you are facing in life.

These scriptures will help you on your journey. For example, if you are facing doubt, search scriptures that deal with doubt. If you are facing fear, search those scriptures. If you are a heavy worrier, search those scriptures. If you are caught up in fornication, see what the scriptures say about that. If you are in adultery, read those scriptures, too. Remember, everything we need is in the Word of God.

JUNE 26

YOU HAVE ALREADY WON THE RACE

...Let us run with patience the race that is set before us.

Hebrews 12:1

We as Christians were already in a race when Jesus rose on the third day with all power. Although you are still running, you must know that your race has already been won. As long as you are living, you will be running for the Lord. Your journey of life is all about God. You may stumble while you are running, but that does not mean you are out of the race. You just need to get back up and keep running with patience.

You may get bruised, hurt, and even be criticized, but just keep running. Don't look back, just keep looking forward. You may feel like giving up, but don't quit. All you need to do is just imagine the finish line; that is when you will meet Jesus "face to face." You will receive your crown of glory. He will be waiting for you and you will be rewarded for your faithfulness, integrity, hard work, diligence, kind acts, etc. He will say, "Well job done, I knew you could do it, my child."

JUNE 27

HAVERST TIME

The harvest is truly plenteous...

Matthew 9:37

During the harvest time a person reaps what they have sown. And when that person has sown a good seed, they can expect a good harvest. Therefore, if you have been committed to God, working tirelessly to do His will, then you better believe that your harvest time is here. Your work was not in vain. It has paid off. You can get ready to receive God's rewards for the seeds that you have sown. This is rightfully yours, so you can get in line.

JUNE 28

STOP DOING TOO MUCH

...Thou art careful and troubled about many things.

Luke 10:41

Some of us are doing too much. If you are this person, then you need to learn to rest. You can become so busy doing everything that you think you can do. You can become stressed and add unnecessary trouble to your life. When a person becomes stressed, it will open the door to complaining. Who wants to be all stressed out? Who thinks that complaining will profit them? I would think no one.

You must be willing to let someone else take charge of certain tasks. I encourage you to get around people who you can trust to help you wholeheartedly. Those people would do just as good of a job as you would do.

JUNE 29

STOP SECOND GUESSING YOURSELF

Be of good cheer...be not afraid.

Matthew 14:27

Some of us will second guess ourselves because we don't have confidence in who we are and what we can do with God on our side. Therefore, we don't believe that we can do certain things. If you are a person who has a habit of second guessing yourself, you need to start having confidence in yourself. If you know within your heart that you can do a certain thing, go for it.

You may want to write a book, but you have been second guessing yourself. You may want to start a business, but you keep second guessing yourself. You may want to be a hair stylist, but you keep second guessing yourself. Think about it. When you second guess yourself, you are in essence second guessing God. When He gives you a strong desire to do a certain thing, you must know that He will make sure He stands behind you, and it will be perfectly done.

JUNE 30

COUNT YOUR BLESSINGS

Ye are blessed of the Lord which made heaven and earth.

Psalm 115:15

You must thank God every single morning, and you have to "count your blessings." One songwriter says, "He keeps on making a way, over and over again." These very words confirm that He continuously pours His blessings upon His children.

We can never stop counting our blessings. Think about it. God has brought you a long way on your journey. You have had some hard times, but He has met every need that you have ever had. You may be in a situation right now, and you need God to send a blessing your way. You can go ahead and expect Him to bless you again and again. It is on the way.

JULY 1

GOD IS YOUR ROADMAP

The steps of a good man are ordered by the Lord...

Psalm 37:23

God is not only your roadmap today; He is your roadmap every day. If you would listen to Him this morning, He will tell you what you need to do first and how you need to end your day. He never steers any of us in the wrong direction. Of course, we can take different routes because some of us are too stubborn or think we know what's really around the next block. God never wants us to go to places where there is danger, so that is why we must follow His leading. I encourage you to let Him take charge of your life today. You can never make it on your life's journey without God as your roadmap.

JULY 2

GET RID OF YOUR OLD WAYS

...Put off concerning the former conversation the old man, which is corrupt according to the deceitful lusts...

Ephesians 4:22

You have to get rid of your old ways just like you throw away food that has been stored in your refrigerator for a few days or so. If you eat spoiled food you can potentially get physically sick. Likewise, if you continue to operate with a carnal mind you can get spiritually sick as time progresses.

You will not be able to handle circumstances as they come your way. Your spirit man will be too weak because your mind has not been fully renewed. I have heard people say, "I used to be like that, but I am not the same person you knew back then..." Usually you can tell if a person is not the same if you stick around for a while. You can tell if they have a renewed mind by their lifestyle.

JULY 3

THAT'S WHY YOU ARE CHOSEN

...Thou art an holy people unto the Lord thy God: the Lord thy God hath chosen thee to be a special people unto himself...

Deuteronomy 7:6

You are chosen because God picked you out of the crowd a long time ago. He knows what you are capable of doing through Him. Because you are a chosen vessel, you have an anointing to help those who long for a spiritual connection with Him.

God may have very well called you to be a preacher, a teacher, a prophet, an evangelist, or to do something else. Don't ever think that you are chosen by a man or a woman. God chose you. He wants you to do His will and walk upright. Today, you need to know that you are special to Him.

JULY 4

KEEP WALKING UPRIGHT

"Whoso walketh uprightly shall be saved..."

Proverbs 28:18

No matter what anybody says to you, just keep walking upright before our Lord and Savior. When you are an upright person, others will be blessed by your presence. You have to always think in terms of doing what is right. There are many things that you can get into in a day's time that can steer you in a direction that is not pointing toward God. You want to keep moving in the right direction so that you can continue receiving everything that Gad has for you.

JULY 5

GOD IS THE DELIVERER

...The Lord is my rock, and my fortress, and my deliverer.

2 Samuel 22:2

God is the One who can deliver us from anything and everything. Who wants to stay in bondage all of their life? I would certainly think that no one would want to be confined year after year. Take a look around you. Many people in your family, among your friends, your church family, and your co-workers have been delivered from bondage. And if you are in bondage that means you can be delivered, too.

You can read the Bible and find out how people who were in bondage were delivered. One interesting book in the Bible that you may want to start reading is Exodus. It shares how God used Moses to help deliver the children of Israel. Don't ever think that God enjoys you being in bondage.

JULY 6

HAVE A BALANCED DAY

And he rested on the seventh day from all his work which he had made.

Genesis 2:2

Many of us try to keep up with today's schedule, tomorrow's schedule, and even what's on the agenda for next week or next month. This in and of itself can bring about imbalance. There is just not enough mind space to hold two, three or more days' worth of "things to do." If you are this person who has been trying to do too much in a day, you need to slow down.

You have to learn the importance of balance. You cannot get everything done in a day. God did not even create the world in a day. It takes time to sort out things and put them in perspective. You have to make sure you have everything prioritized. Today, just take your time to do what is on your agenda for this day. Always make sure you put God first.

JULY 7

GOD WILL MAKE PROVISION FOR THE VISION

Where there is no vision, the people perish...

Proverbs 29:18

God will certainly make provision for the vision He gives to each of us. If He has already shown you something that He wants you to do, even if it appears to be huge, I want to encourage you today to hold on to that vision. If it hasn't fully manifested in your life, just know that it will never diminish.

You must believe that. All you need to do is continue watering your vision with faith. And always be mindful of who you share it with because it cannot be shared with everyone, those members of your family, and even some of your church members.

JULY 8

CLEAN UP YOUR WAYS

All the ways of a man is clean in his own life; but the Lord weigheth the spirits.

Proverbs 16:2

Are you happy with the way you are in life? Would you say that your ways are good or nasty? Be honest with yourself. If you said that your ways are good, then I want to encourage you to keep being the person you are. You will continue to positively impact those who you may come in contact with daily.

If you think your ways are nasty, then you need to be polished from the crown of your head to the sole of your feet. You have to realize that people will withdraw from you when you have such nasty ways. You are going to have to look in the mirror today and sincerely ask God to change your ways. Trust me; He will certainly do it for you.

JULY 9

BE A SERVANT RATHER THAN A SERPENT

But he that is greatest among you shall be your servant.

Matthew 23:11

When you are a servant you will gladly help people without seeking something in return. You will feed those who are hungry, encourage those who are weak, bless someone with a financial seed, etc.

Likewise, when you act as a serpent {snake}, you will do anything to hurt people. For example, if you don't like your coworker, you will purposely try to get them fired. If you don't like your church member, you will be open to witchcraft. If you are tired of your mate, you will freely cheat on them. You don't have a care in the world when you act as a serpent.

JULY 10

COUNT IT ALL JOY

"My brethren, count it all joy when ye fall into divers temptation."

James 1:2

You must learn to count it all joy when you come up against the devil's snares. Count it all joy when the devil uses someone to gossip about you, pray against you, and just hate you because of your existence. Don't let any of these things steal your joy because you have God on your side.

The devil cannot and will not control your life, not even with the temptations he presents to you. Those things that I mentioned can easily make you lose yourself and retaliate, but always remember that God will "fight your battle."

JULY 11

KEEP GOD'S COMMANDMENTS

I am the Lord thy God, which have brought thee out of the land of Egypt...thou shalt not have no other gods before me...

Exodus 20:2

There are lists of commandments in the Bible that we all should be following. If you are not following these commandments that are outlined, then you may want to practice executing them. Let us make sure that we are not committing any form of adultery.

We should always be mindful that there is only One God, so let us not get into serving any false gods. If something doesn't belong to you, then you shouldn't steal it. God has something for you, too. Since you didn't give life, don't take anyone's life. These are just a few commandments that I wanted to highlight. Read Exodus, Chapter 20 to learn of the others.

JULY 12

RESPECT EVERYONE

God looked upon the children of Israel, and God had respect unto them.

Exodus 2:25

You should not only have respect for those few people who are in your circle, but you should learn to have respect for everyone. Having respect for yourself and others will carry you so far in life. People will have a tendency to remember you just because of how respectful you are.

Have you ever noticed when some people come to work, meeting, or some other gathering and only speak to certain people? This is not only rude when a person does this; it simply shows how much respect that person has for those who they don't speak to. If you have been guilty of this act, I encourage you to start being mindful of others, showing respect as Jesus would do.

JULY 13

BE TENACIOUS

Arise, and go into the city, and it shall be told thee what thou must do.

Acts 9:6

You keep being tenacious and doing what you are doing for the Lord. The more you try to do right, wrong will continue to stare you in the face. But don't partake in the wrong. Don't let anyone take you off course. Don't easily be moved by what is going on around you. Be on fire for the things of God. Let Him create in you a clean heart so that you can have a drive to do His will and the tenacity to do what He has purposed you to do. I am certain that you see all kinds of things within a day. As long as you know who your God is and what pleases Him, you continue being the tenacious person you are.

JULY 14

AN APPOINTED TIME

Is anything too hard for God? At the time appointed I will...

Genesis 18:14

You may have heard that "there is an appointed time..." only God knows the appointed time for you to go to the next level, for you to get married, for you to start your ministry, for you to start your business, for you to get that promotion you want, etc. There is no better time than His time. If you can just wait on Him, then you will find yourself being in the "right place at the right time," and in the right season.

JULY 15

BE CAREFUL WHAT YOU HEAR

Cause me to hear thy lovingkindness in the morning...

Psalm 143:8

You have to make sure you protect what goes in your ears daily. Some of what we hear is not always in alignment with the Word of God. Sometimes we may lend our ears to gossip throughout the day. While we are not in a church environment every day, we must still conduct ourselves as children of God.

There are people who are communicating garbage everyday on various social sites. You must protect your ears and learn not to entertain the things that are harmful to your spirit, whether you are directly communicating with a person or read something on one of the social sites that someone has posted.

JULY 16

BE A GOOD SAMARITAN

But a certain Samaritan, as he journeyed, came where he was: and when he saw him, he had compassion on him.

Luke 10:33

You will find that there are people all across the globe that needs a hand up. Many of them are not looking for a "hand out," they just need help to get back on their feet. Many have "fallen by the wayside" due to being in a place of distress. You never know what a person has gone through in their life. So much can happen in a short length of time to set a person back.

Oftentimes when a person is at a low point in their life, they tend to feel very weak. But "the strong ought to bear the infirmities of the weak..." (Romans 15:1). This is where you can become that Good Samaritan, by being there for that person (s).

JULY 17

DON'T PRACTICE EVIL DOINGS

Turn not to the right or to the left: remove thy foot from evil.

Proverbs 4:27

People are practicing all kinds of evil against others. The most common reason is because of hatred, and maybe even jealousy. The Bible clearly instructs us to remove our feet from evil. That means all manners of evil.

If you are having an issue with a person, don't go to someone who performs witchcraft, don't speak evil against people, don't wish or hope something bad happens to a person. Don't despise people because of where they are in their lives. You must make sure that you are doing what is right toward people, treating them kind. Today, I encourage you to always treat others well, no matter how a person treats you.

JULY 18

REMEMBER WHAT YOU SAID THAT YOU WOULD DO WHEN GOD DELIVERS YOU

Giving thanks to unto the Father, which hath made us meet to be partakers of the inheritance of the saints in light: who hath delivered us from the power of darkness...

Colossians 1:12-13

Oftentimes we make God promises and we don't usually follow through with those promises. Many of us will share our excitement with others about what we plan to do when God delivers us from the mess we put ourselves in, but once our deliverance take place, we default on the promises we made to God. Remember, He will never default on His promises that He makes to us.

Some of you have made a promise to give more when God blessed you with a financial increase. Some of you promised that you will go to church when He blessed you to get out of the "sick bed." Some of you also promised God that you were going to help others when He blessed you to become successful. You have to remember what you told God that you would do. Start keeping the promises you make to God.

JULY 19

LET'S REMEMBER WHO CAME BEFORE US

I am come that they might have life, and that they might have it more abundantly.

John 10:10

Each of us should never forget who came before us—Jesus Christ, the Holy One. He came to fulfill a major purpose, and that was to die for the remission of our sins. You will learn what He did while here on earth if you pick up your Bible and start reading the book of Matthew in the New Testament.

We all have been assigned by God to fulfill a purpose while we are here on earth, too. The One who came before us can help us make a difference in the world. And He lives on the inside of us; therefore, "we can change the world."

JULY 20

OBEDIENCE BRINGS BLESSINGS

If ye be willing and obedient, ye shall eat the good of the land

Isaiah 1:19

When you are obedient to God, you can welcome blessings. The blessings are rightfully yours. Your territory can expand more when you are willing to do what God tells you to do. We must obey His Word every day.

When God blesses you, it is not limited to the material things. The material things are what a lot of people pray for. But you can receive spiritual blessings as well. What I mean by this is that you can receive a greater level of anointing. You can receive a greater level of faith, and so much more.

JULY 21

THE NAME OF JESUS

"O Lord, our Lord, how excellent is thy name in all the earth! Who hast set they glory above the heavens."

Psalm 8:1

The name of Jesus is excellent. It truly exceeds every name there is. It is above every name. It is a powerful name. It is a faithful name. It is a loving name. It is an awesome name. It is a merciful name. It is a name that if called upon, will make demons tremble. Try calling His name today. You can find out just how excellent His name is when you call Him at any time of day or night. He will answer you. He even answered you when you were doing wrong. You were all in the devil's territory and He answered you and rescued you, too.

JULY 22

DON'T LOOK BACK

Escape for they life; look not behind thee...

Genesis 19:17

There are some places that you can no longer frequent. If you have experienced freedom, you must not look behind you. Don't go back and start doing those things again. According to the Bible, the Lord clearly gave Lot instructions to leave Sodom, because He was about to destroy that city, and Gomorrah, because of all the wickedness and sin that was going on. When Lot's wife looked back she had turned into "a pillar of salt." This should show you that things can become hard in your life when you go back to your old ways.

JULY 23

STRIVE FOR PERFECTION

...Let us go on unto perfection...

Hebrews 6:1

If you are a person who is accustomed to saying, "I am not perfect," you need to rephrase what you are saying. Why don't you start saying, "I am striving for perfection each day. I want to live a holy life." You can't get to perfection alone, but as long as your desire for perfection exists, God will help you.

You can no longer make excuses to sin because of your imperfections. You have to make a decision to do what is right all the time. God sees when you are striving. I want to encourage you to continue in the direction of walking upright before Him.

JULY 24

GO FORWARD

...And ye shall go forth, and grow...

Malachi 4:2

So many people find themselves going backward in life. If you have come to a stopping point and are confused about whether or not you should go back to that job that you were released from or that marriage that you were released from or any other situation God delivered you from, you must know that it is time to move forward. God is propelling you to a new dimension.

You can go forward with "a smile on your face, a Holy Ghost dance, a shout in your spirit, and praise on your lips." There is a wonderful place in God for you, and your assignment that He has for you to do requires movement. You can't stop now. The amazing thing is that you can start moving forward today.

JULY 25

DRAW CLOSER TO GOD

"Draw nigh to God, and he will draw nigh to you."

James 4:8

Are you ready to draw closer to God? Do you know that He wants you to fill His presence right when you step foot out of your bed. Just thank Him this morning. Welcome Him in your home, your car, your job atmosphere, etc. Share with your friends and family about His goodness. Give Him your full attention today. He knows when you are putting Him first, and He loves that. You can draw closer and closer each day. You don't have to let anyone or anything keep you from getting closer to your Heavenly Father.

JULY 26

GOD WILL REVEAL IT TO YOU

...Lord of kings, and a revealer of secrets, seeing thou couldest reveal this secret.

Daniel 2:47

What is it that you want God to reveal to you? Whether you are with the right mate, at the right job, or something else, God will reveal whatever it is that you want to know. You have to trust Him. It will be in His timing, but it will be revealed to you. So don't become too anxious and let your mind entertain the thought of going to a psychic or a soothsayer. God is the only One you need to reach out to. Some of the things He reveals to you may not be to your liking. It may hurt, but God is the comforter; therefore, it is okay.

JULY 27

BE HOLY

"Because it is written, be ye holy; for I am holy."

1Peter 1:16

God wants us to be holy all the time because we are His children. He is holy all the time; therefore, we can't just be holy on Sunday's when we are in church. That would be considered as being holy part-time. If you want God to use you all the time, you have to willing to be perfected. You have to get from around people who are trying to get you to contaminate your temple {body}. You don't want to do that which will hinder you from being holy. You can come out of darkness and let God clean you up today.

JULY 28

DON'T REJOICE OVER SOMEONE'S FAILURES

"Rejoice not when thine enemy falleth: and let not thine heart be glad when he stumbleth."

Proverbs 24:17

I am certain that there are people who don't like you, and many of them may have purposely tried to hurt you. You must understand that everyone is not going to be a friend to you. Some people will serve as your enemy. They are on the devil's team. But even in spite of that, you should never rejoice if they fail or come to a hard place in their life. Instead, you should pray them, asking God to have grace and mercy on them. This is the right thing to do, especially when you are a Christian.

JULY 29

THE BLOOD OF JESUS

..The blood of Jesus Christ his Son cleanseth us from all sin.

1 John 1:7

One thing that you have to understand is that the blood of Jesus Christ has unlimited power. We Christians were purchased with the blood He shed on Calvary. As you start the day off and thank God for waking you, ask Him to cover you with His blood as you travel to work or wherever else you plan to go.

There is nothing that can touch you or harm you when you are covered in His blood. Don't let anyone tell you differently. You can command the devil and His demons to flee by the blood of Jesus.

JULY 30

PLANT YOUR SEED AND WALK AWAY

For the seed shall be prosperous.

Zechariah 8:12

When you plant a seed you don't have to stand there and watch it grow, you can walk away. Whatever seed you plant, it will grow over a period of time. You need to make sure it is a good seed, because that is what will be produced. Any form of bad seeds will produce bad results. Today, make sure you plant that which will produce a rewarding harvest. It is a joyful moment when receiving a harvest that was well worth waiting for.

JULY 31

BE EAGER TO LEARN SOMETHING NEW

Learn to do well...

Isaiah 1:17

How does it make you feel when you learn something new? I have learned that when you have an eagerness to learn something new, you will do your best. You won't need much training because of that inner desire. You will catch on pretty quickly. When you learn something new it is not just limited to what you do at work. You can learn how to do something new around the house, and even at church. It is just something about newness. Why don't you try learning something new today?

AUGUST 1

FORGET ABOUT YESTERDAY; LIVE IN TODAY

For a thousand years in thy sight are but as yesterday when it is past...

Psalm 90:4

Too often we can focus on what happened on yesterday, but we have to leave yesterday behind us and live in today. There are brand new opportunities that were not presented to you on yesterday. You must remember that yesterday is your past. God does not want you to focus on yesterday because He wants you to receive your miracle, your breakthrough, understanding, a new direction, a new level of discernment and much more today.

AUGUST 2

GIVE RESPECT AND RECEIVE RESPECT

And as ye would that men should do to you, do ye also to them likewise.

Luke 6:31

Anytime you give respect to a person, you will receive respect from that person. Let's not make excuses for being disrespectful. Be careful to continue treating those who do not like you with the utmost respect, even if they don't reciprocate. Make sure you bless that brother or sister that disrespected you, and show love to everyone. It is not about you today; it is about God having His way through you.

AUGUST 3

GET OFF COMFORT STREET

...we cannot be satisfied.

Job 31:31

I like to say when people are too comfortable they are traveling down Comfort Street. What I mean by this is that some people enjoy where they are mentally, emotionally, socially and spiritually. If you are one of those people, I want to tell you that there is so much more to life; therefore, you can make a decision today to get off Comfort Street. I don't believe that God wants us Christians to become too comfortable. He has an assignment for each of us to execute, and in order for us to fulfill our assignment, we can't get comfortable. It's time to work.

AUGUST 4

I BESEECH YOU LORD

O Lord, I beseech the, deliver my soul.

Psalm 116:4

When you read the book of Psalm, you will find that David was one who poured His heart out to God. He said, "I beseech the..." You may have gotten yourself into a lot of mess, and you need God to move speedily in your life. You need to be delivered from various things. And today you can be delivered.

You just need to go to God with an open heart, and tell Him, "I beseech you, Lord. I need you to straighten some things out in my life. I know that you are the only One who can do it. I need deliverance right now."

AUGUST 5

TITHE BEYOND MONEY

...Freely ye have received, freely give.

Matthew 10:8

I am certain that many of you are always prepared to pay your tithes on Sunday mornings. Tithing is a requirement according to the Bible. It is 10% portion of what we Christians earn on a weekly, bi-weekly or monthly basis. But I am convinced that we can tithe beyond money. You can give someone a smile, a laugh, a kind word, a handshake, a listening ear, etc. When you develop a giving mentality you will gladly give money as well as other small tokens that are often appreciated. Today, I encourage you to tithe beyond money.

AUGUST 6

ARE YOU THIRSTY?

But whosoever drinketh of the water that I shall give shall never thirst...

Luke 4:14

Have you ever been thirsty for water, your favorite soda, or juice? I am certain that you quenched your thirst with water, your favorite soda, or something else. I want to ask today, "Are you thirsty for God?" If your answer is "Yes," I want you to know that you can quench the thirst in your soul with His presence, His love, His heart, His mind, and His Word. He can fill every void in your life. You don't have to be thirsty another day.

AUGUST 7

SEE THROUGH YOUR SPIRITUAL EYES

Having eyes, see ye not?

Mark 8:18

Some things in life can only be detected through our spiritual eyes. If you try to look at your situations and circumstances through your natural eyes, you will totally miss it. If God arrange some things in your life that is for your good, please don't try to understand with your natural mind and see it through your natural eyes.

You will have to get in the spirit in order to grasp it, and you will only be able to see it with your spiritual eyes. A lot of things that happen in our lives we think are bad, but those things are really good. I want you to know today that everything that is happening in your life is all "for your good."

AUGUST 8

GOD IS NOT DONE YET

Make me to go in the path of thy commandments; for therein do I delight.

Psalm 119:35

I have heard many people say, "God is not done with me yet." I don't believe that God is done with any of us yet. We are not perfect beings. With that being said, we still have some things in our lives that need to be worked out. You can just relinquish your will over to God's will today.

When God is done with you, you will be totally happy with the finish product. You will be able to walk in your purpose and shine before nations. You will always know that there is so much more that God will do through you and for you as you continue to walk in your purpose. He is always working on His beloved children. That is why you have to be more patient with people who may not have arrived to where you are in your life.

AUGUST 9

DON'T BE WASTEFUL

*...Give an account of thy stewardship...for my lord taketh away
from me the stewardship.*

Luke 16:2-3

A lot of us waste our time, our mind, our money, etc. If you know that you have been wasteful, you have an opportunity today to show appreciation for everything that God has blessed you with. The time that you have in a day does not need to be wasted. The food that you are blessed to eat does not need to be wasted. The money that God has blessed you with does not need to be wasted. The mind that He has given you to think clearly and wisely does not need to be wasted.

You must be mindful of the way you handle your resources. God is looking for those who are going to be good stewards over what He has blessed them with. Going forward, you must learn how to handle what God has given you and make sure you are not being wasteful.

AUGUST 10

DON'T BURY YOUR TALENTS

And unto one he gave five talents, to another two, and to another one; to every man according to his several ability...

Matthew 25:15

The talents that God gave you are to be used to His glory. You should not bury them. Some of you may have one or more. If you have a talent to style hair beautifully, you should go for it. If you have a talent to fix cars, go ahead and get the necessary credentials, the tools, and start doing it. If you have a talent to sing, start participating in singing competitions. You can even record at home and upload it on the internet. If you know how to act, go ahead and start pursuing it. Don't continue burying your talents. Start today!

AUGUST 11

DON'T BETRAY PEOPLE

Verily I say unto you, that one of you shall betray me.

Matthew 26:21

The Bible tells us that Jesus was betrayed by Judas. While this was a negative act on Judas' part, this betrayal led Jesus Christ to the cross to make the ultimate sacrifice for all of us. Judas had to deal with the consequences after betraying Jesus. The aftermath of this betrayal led Judas to kill himself.

When you betray people it leaves them in a place of distrust. They will less likely trust someone else. Well, at least for a while. You could very well be one of those people who have been betrayed. If this is you, how did it make you feel when you were betrayed by someone? I am certain that you thought the person who betrayed you had your best interest at heart, but after the betrayal you realized they didn't. You cannot expect to do someone wrong and receive something good behind it.

AUGUST 12

AGREE WITH SOMEONE IN PRAYER

Again I say unto you, that if two of you shall agree on earth as touching anything that they shall ask, it shall be done for them of my Father which is in heaven.

Matthew 18:19

Today, you can agree with someone in prayer. Your mother, father, child, sister, friend, or even a co-worker may need you to be in agreement with them about something they could be facing right now. I am certain that you have heard that there is "power in prayer."

How much more powerful it is when there are two or more people praying about a matter? This is what some would describe as a "unity prayer." According to the Bible, whatever they ask, it shall be done. You must have faith that God will answer your prayers when you offer them unto Him.

AUGUST 13

MAKE ME OVER

Wash you, make you clean...

Isaiah 1:16

You may have seen on television where a man or woman received a makeover. Some of them have a serious cosmetic surgery to change their appearance. When you take a look at the before and after picture, you can see the major difference in their appearance.

One songwriter says, "Make me over..." I want to tell you that God wants to do a serious makeover on you today. He wants to transform your mind and clean up your heart so that your spirit can be refreshed. The makeover that He gives you will make you better on the inside as well as the outside. You don't have to pay a dime for this makeover as one would do to enhance their outer appearance. Tell God that you desire a makeover today, and He will start on it right away.

AUGUST 14

THE FLOODS OF LIFE CAN'T SWEEP YOU AWAY

...When the enemy shall come in like a flood, the Spirit of the Lord shall lift up a standard against him."

Isaiah 59:19

One thing you must remember is that when the enemy comes into your life like a flood, those floods of life will not be able to sweep you away because you are covered by the blood of Jesus Christ. The Word of God says that "the Lord shall lift up a standard..." With that being said, you should have confidence in knowing that no matter what kind of hell you are going through, you will be taken care of when those floods come to try to sweep you away. Whatever the enemy tries, it will not work.

AUGUST 15

LEARN HOW TO RECOGNIZE THE DEVIL'S TRICKS

...Satan hath desired to have you, that he may sift you as wheat.

Luke 22:31

I once heard a pastor say, "The devil isn't using any new tricks..." How many of you believe that? I do. Every once in a while the enemy will come with the same trick he used maybe a year or two ago. Although he is crafty, he is not wise at all. Therefore, we as Christians must use the wisdom that God has given to us to study the enemy's tricks so that when he comes with them again, we can call him out.

We can tell him, "I know what you are trying to do Satan, but it won't work, now "Get thee behind me..." He may very well try to come with one of those tricks today. Make sure you stay in your prayer zone. Make sure you keep your spiritual eyes opened at all times.

AUGUST 16

STAY LINKED TO GOOD PEOPLE

A good man out of the good treasure of the heart bringeth forth good things...

Matthew 12:35

You will find as you stay linked to good people, you will draw strength from them. Although there is an inner strength that each of us has, there is always good to draw that additional strength and energy from those good people in your circle. When you are around good people, they will help thrust you into your purpose. They will pray with you, encourage you, and share with you.

If you have ever experienced having bad people in your circle, I am certain that over time you felt the negative vibes. These people are only negative influences; they can release so much negative energy that you will find yourself not being able to thrive spiritually or physically. Your thoughts will be based upon things that they have said or done. You will not have the courage to even move forward with the plans that God has for your life. I encourage you to eliminate the negative people in your circle and stay linked to the good ones.

AUGUST 17

HAVE GOOD MOTIVES

A merciful man doeth good to his own soul...

Proverbs 11:17

You should always have good motives. I want to tell you to stop trying to con people. Stop thinking of only you! This is a brand new day, and you can start it off right by telling yourself that you are going to treat everyone good and have the right motives.

When any of us have bad motives we will find that they will backfire on us. No one can expect to receive the blessings of God when they have an evil mindset. Whether you know it or not, when a person has bad motives, they are practicing evil doings.

AUGUST 18

EXPECT GOD TO DO SOMETHING GREAT

My soul, wait thou only upon God; for my expectation is from him.

Psalm 62:5

Some of us operate in so much fear, and we think pessimistic. We as Christians should always expect great things to happen to us, for us, and through us. We need to have hearts of expectancy; therefore, we will become more optimistic.

As you start your day this morning, you need to tell God that you are expecting for Him to do something uncommon in your life today. Believe me, God wants to do so many greats things in your life—things that don't make sense to the average human. Sometimes He does things that will blow everyone's mind. This shows how great God is alone, and nothing can ever be compared to what He does for any of us. Today, I encourage you to put your seatbelt on and expect something from God that will be out of the norm. You are going to know that it was only Him that did it.

AUGUST 19

WHAT ARE YOU SEEKING?

...seek and ye shall find

Matthew 7:7

What are you seeking? Are you seeking happiness? Are you seeking joy? Are you seeking peace? Are you seeking comfort? Are you seeking approval? Are you seeking a miracle? Are you seeking wisdom? Are you seeking a job? Are you seeking a mate? Are you seeking a closer relationship with God? Are you seeking a church home to fellowship with sincere men and women of God?

You must learn today that whatever you are seeking, it is in God. He can help you. His word says, "Seek and ye shall find." But, guess what? Luke 12:31 says, "...seek the kingdom of God; and all these things shall be added unto you. This scripture alone should give you the assurance that whatever you are seeking, it will be given unto you when you seek God's kingdom.

AUGUST 20

DON'T COMPARE

...I am fearfully and wonderfully made...

Psalm 139:14

Some of us can get so comfortable with comparing our children to other children, our spouse with someone else's spouse, our pastor with other pastors, etc. This is something that we need to stop, starting today. Those are your children that God gave you, so appreciate them. That is your spouse that God gave you, so appreciate him or her. God placed you under your pastor, so thank God for him or her. Don't compare them with anyone else.

You must understand that people don't like to be compared to other people. God made each one of us uniquely different, and he gave each one of us different talents and gifts. In my opinion, I don't think it is ever right to compare people. It is a different scenario when comparing things.

AUGUST 21

DON'T GET TOO COMPLACENT

Grow in grace, and in the knowledge of our Lord and Savior Jesus Christ...

2 Peter 3:18

Some of us are too familiar with complacency. You should never be too satisfied with where you are because there is always room for growth in every part of your life. You have to be willing to come out of your comfort zone and go higher in the Lord. He has mighty things for you to do. When you are a complacent person, then you will have a tendency to settle for less on your job, in your ministry, in your home, etc. God does not want any of us to have the settling mentality. It is time to go higher and higher in God.

AUGUST 22

SPEAK TO ME LORD

He spake unto them in the cloudy pillar...

Psalm 99:7

God is always speaking to us. You just have to get to that place of peace so that you will hear clearly what He is saying. There are small details that you can easily miss when you are not in a listening mode. When that still small voice softly speaks in your ear, telling you to act right, you must know that is God.

When you are traveling down the road and that voice tells you to turn left instead of going straight, you must know that is God. When you are about to argue with your spouse and that voice tells you to love your spouse, you must know that is God. When you start yelling at your children and that voice tells you to be quiet, you must know that is God.

AUGUST 23

GOD IS MARVELOUS

Blessed the Lord: for he hath shewed me hi marvelous kindness...

Psalm 31:21

God continues to show us how marvelous He is. If you are alive today, then you ought to be grateful. This in and of itself shows us what kind of God we serve. Some of you may be in a trial right now, but He wants you to trust Him with every ounce of your being. He is honored to bring you out of that situation, man of God. He marvels at how you been handling the situation, woman of God. Today, I encourage you to keep your eyes on the marvelous One—God Almighty!

AUGUST 24

CHALLENGE YOURSELF

...Endure hardness, as a good soldier of Jesus Christ.

2 Timothy 2:3

You don't have to always be in a position for other people to challenge you. At times we have to challenge ourselves. It is very necessary that we do this because when we don't challenge ourselves, we can become too lazy. We will find ourselves saying, "It's too hard. I can't do that."

Just know that if you can meet certain challenges, you can become a stronger person; it shows that inner strength that you have. Today, I want you to do something that seems difficult and follow through with it no matter how hard it seems.

AUGUST 25

SHAKE IT OFF

...Let every man be swift to hear, slow to speak, slow to wrath...

James 1:19

You may find yourself having to shake some things off. This wouldn't be a bad idea when you think about how quickly the spirit of anger, jealousy, gossip, confusion, among many other things, can creep up on you. Be encouraged and don't give into any of these spirits today.

Don't you know that the devil and his demons rejoice when you operate in the spirit of anger...he wants to block any blessings that God has in store for you. You may have to shake something off every day, but it will be better for that "something" to be off you rather than on you.

AUGUST 26

DON'T BE HASTY

Be not hasty to go out of his sight...

Ecclesiastes 8:3

Many of us will step out of God's presence when we haste to do things. We must always consult God before we make any kind of decision. Although we want things to manifest in our lives instantly, God does have the perfect time for things to happen in our favor. Today, if you know that you are hasting to do something, just think and pray about it, and then let God lead you every step of the way. Don't allow the adversary to confuse you nor tell you that the time is now.

AUGUST 27

BE READY

Therefore be ye also ready...

Matthew 24:44

All of God's children should be ready for the things of God. Your mind should be focused on blessing someone today. You may have to minister to someone. You may have to just listen to someone. You may even have to feed someone. Either way, you just need to be ready. You never know where the end is at for you, and what you do for God is what really matters.

God will forever commission His children to do things that will glorify Him. He wants to work through you. I want you to think about this: People who are committed are seemingly the ones who are ready. They are ready for whatever God has for them to do.

AUGUST 28

YOU ARE CERTIFIED AND QUALIFIED

Before I formed thee in thy belly I knew thee...

Jeremiah 1:5

You may have been applying for a job that requires a certification, along with a long list of other credentials. You must know that God can grant you the job without having those certifications. He has already certified and qualified you once you received Him in your heart. So, the favor will cause you to have things without the requirements of the worldly system.

Remember, there isn't a long list of things you have to do to become certified and qualified as a child of God. All you have to do is accept Jesus as your Lord and Savior. When you accept Him, you are covered by His blood. You are partners with Him. You will receive everything you need.

AUGUST 29

RELAX YOUR MIND

Be renewed in the spirit of your mind.

Ephesians 4:23

We have to come to that place of relaxation daily. Our mind and body need to rest from a busy day's work. Some of you are used to working eight to twelve hours a day. And some of you exceed those working hours in a day. When you get off work you need to go straight home and relax your mind.

If someone calls you about hanging out or doing something else, you need to tell them that you are going home to get some rest. It may take some of you to relax in order for you to realize just how tired you are mentally and physically. In order to do what is needed for God, you have to be rested; therefore, you know you need to be rested while doing other things.

AUGUST 30

DON'T THROW IN THE TOWEL

Trust in the Lord with all thine heart; and lean not unto thine own understanding.

Proverbs 3:5

You may feel like just throwing in the towel because you don't trust God. Just because you have seen other people quit, does not mean that you have to throw in the towel. You have a lot to look forward to. Anytime someone gives up, it means that they may not have the faith they need to follow through with what they have started. This could be coupled with many other things as well.

Some people quit because they don't believe in themselves. I want to encourage you today to stay focused on what you are doing. Don't give up so easily. You have a good reason to keep moving forward in life.

AUGUST 31

KEEP SOME MATTERS CONFIDENTIAL

See, thou tell no man; but go thy way....

Matthew 8:4

Has anyone ever told you something in confidence and you shared it with someone else? You must learn to keep some matters confidential. When someone confides in you, that means they trust that you will pray about it and offer whatever solution you may have. If they wanted someone else to know about an important matter, don't you think they would have told them?

There are a lot of hurting people in the world who have not yet accepted Jesus in their life, and they need to talk to and confide in us Christians who are not going to "spill the beans," but spill the truth about Jesus.

SEPTEMBER 1

ARE YOU WEARING YOUR HELMET OF SALVATION?

And take the helmet of salvation...

Ephesians 6:17

We Christians are in a constant spiritual battle. The Bible encourages us to put on the whole armour of God. The helmet of salvation is part of this armour. It will help protect your head {the mind} while in battle. Sometimes the battle can be only in the mind. You may deal with negative thoughts all day long. The enemy will try to steal your joy and peace with these thoughts.

I want to encourage you to gear up with the helmet of salvation as you prepare to step foot out of your door this morning. You must always remember that our adversary is going to throw things your way. You are not exempt when you are a child of God from the devil's attacks. Whether you recognize the devil' attacks or not, his mission is still to destroy you.

SEPTEMBER 2

KEEP ON YOUR BREASTPLATE OF RIGHTEOUSNESS

...Having on the breastplate of righteousness...

Ephesians 6:14

You must also keep on your breastplate of righteousness. This is another part of God's armour. You have to protect your heart. You don't want it to be contaminated with evil. Just imagine a soldier fighting in a war. He or she has to have on something that will protect them from head to toe. That which covers their chest will help block wounds to the chest.

We Christians must think in terms of this when we are in a spiritual battle with the enemy every day. The devil wants to catch us off guard, not wearing our armour so that he can try to destroy us with his fiery darts. I encourage you to always keep on your breastplate of righteousness. I am certain that you can tell the difference when not wearing it, right?

SEPTEMBER 3

DON'T BE CRAFTY

...Not walking in craftiness, nor handling the word of God deceitfully...

2 Corinthians 4:2

If you have anything deceitful on your mind this morning, you need to ask God to erase it right now. You cannot expect to be blessed and be crafty at the same time. God does not reward people for their wrong doing.

When a person is crafty they are allowing Satan to use them to take advantage of someone, plot against someone, attack someone's character, etc. If you find yourself doing any of these things, you need to repent and turn from it. You can do good things today.

SEPTEMBER 4

GOD IS LONGSUFFERING

...The Lord God, merciful and gracious, longsuffering, and abundant in goodness and truth.

Exodus 34:6

Did you know that God is longsuffering? The Bible mentions the longsuffering of God quite often. When I think of His longsuffering, I think of how many chances He gives to His loving children. He bears with us "time after time." It seems as though some of you don't want to get it right. You continue to do wrong, and God has been just standing there saying, "Hey, how long are you willing to disobey me? I have extended my grace and mercy to you. I love you my child."

Now that is what I call longsuffering. If you think about doing a person wrong for a long period of time, you should know that the person will get tired. And they will give up on you. However, God will never give up on you because He is longsuffering. I want to encourage you to line up according to God's will. Don't go another day taking advantage of His mercy and grace.

SEPTEMBER 5

HAVE CONFIDENCE

For the Lord shall be thy confidence...

Proverbs 3:26

You should always have confidence in yourself. When a person lacks confidence, it will show in everything they do. They will be reluctant to do things that can possibly help them. The excuses will come one after another when someone doesn't believe in their ability to do something in life that someone may have told them they could never do.

You can no longer make excuses. You cannot entertain anything negative that is spoken against you. God has given you everything you need to succeed in life. You must have the faith in knowing that He will guide you through any task you embark on. You should always have a high level of confidence, especially knowing that you have the Great I Am walking alongside you every day.

SEPTEMBER 6

ESTEEM OTHERS

...Let each esteem others better than themselves.

Philippians 2:3

Some of us tear people down with what we say to them. Interestingly, some of us don't have a care in this world of how we hurt people. God is not glorified by when we discourage or gossip or criticize others. He is glorified when we esteem others.

If you have been guilty of tearing others down, you can start this day by saying positive things that will make someone smile. People thrive when they hear people say good things about them. God encourages us to uplift each other. You can start today.

SEPTEMBER 7

RELEASE THE BAD HABITS

He delivered me from my strong enemy...

2 Samuel 22:18

You may have been holding on to some bad habits for many years. Don't you know that a bad habit is your enemy? It is time to make a 360 degree turn. You can start making this turn in your life on this day. Guess what? God will help you. Just simply say, "I don't want to be a part of this anymore, I am tired, I am no longer happy with this in my life, and I am ready to release it."

Now if you really mean what you just said, you can go ahead and make room for something new. The bad habits will start shifting. The craving is about to diminish. Those habits can no longer have your mind. They will start being the least of importance in your life, no matter what the habit is.

SEPTEMBER 8

BE A PEACE MAKER

Blessed are the peacemakers: for they shall be called the children of God.

Matthew 5:9

Do you like starting confusion? Do you know of someone who keeps confusion going? Don't you know that God loves peace? He wants us to live and lead a peaceful life. When you experience peace it is easier for you to be a peacemaker. You will go the opposite direction of trouble. You can let peace spill over into your home, your job, your church and everywhere else you tread your feet today.

SEPTEMBER 9

SELFISHNESS IS NOT GOOD

As we have therefore opportunity, let us do good unto all men, especially unto them who are of the household of faith.

Galatians 6:10

When you only think of yourself it can become very challenging for you. It is not good to always think of your needs; you should think of how you can extend a helping hand to someone else. Don't you know that it is not all about you?

You can start today by thinking of ways to be a blessing to others. Just take a moment to say, "I am going to do this for him today." I am going to buy her lunch today." When you do things like this, these are counted as good deeds in Jesus' book. You are showing through your actions that you are not selfish.

SEPTEMBER 10

DON'T BE LUSTFUL

Walk in the Spirit, and ye shall not fulfill the lust of the flesh.

Galatians 5:16

Child of God, your flesh will crave that which is not good for you. You must tell your flesh to "get back in line!" You don't have to please your flesh. Your primary goal should be to please your Heavenly Father. Your flesh can get you in so much trouble. I have one question for you: Do you like getting in trouble?

Today, you can make up your mind that you are going to think about that which is pleasing unto to God. You will find that when your thoughts are placed upon heavenly things, then you will have less time to yield to your flesh. Remember, you have to cast down those thoughts that are detrimental to your flesh. Don't carry out those thoughts if they are not in alignment with the Word of God.

SEPTEMBER 11

REPENT FOR YOUR SINS

For sin shall not have dominion over you...

Romans 6:14

We must repent daily for our sins. We have all sinned at some point in our lives, but we must always remember that it is never God's will for us to willfully sin. He does not tempt any of us to do wrong. He wants us to live a holy life.

You must declare this day forward that you will steer away from sin when it seeks you out. You have to talk to your situation and tell your flesh that you are not going to succumb to any form of sin. You must repent and turn in a different direction. There are so many other things that you can be doing instead of sinning. Today, ask God to order your steps.

SEPTEMBER 12

HAPPINESS IS ON THE INSIDE OF YOU

But the Comforter, which is the Holy Ghost, whom the Father will send in my name, he shall teach you all things, and bring all things to your remembrance, whatsoever I have said unto you.

John 14:26

Many of us depend on other people to make us happy. Some of us feel that things can make us happy. Instead of looking for people and things to make you happy, you should search deep within. That is where you will find happiness. The Holy Spirit lives on the inside of you, and He is in essence happiness.

He is your comforter, your peace, your protection, just to name a few. You should always remember that people will let you down, but God won't. He will not steal your joy and happiness. You don't have to go another day thinking that happiness is anywhere outside of you; therefore, you don't have to search for it.

SEPTEMBER 13

LET'S BEGIN AND STOP PROCRASTINATING

Slothfulness casteth into a deep sleep: an idle soul shall suffer hunger.

Proverbs 19:15

Do you ever find yourself procrastinating? Procrastination can become your enemy if you allow it to. At some point you have to put into action what your heart has been telling you to do, and God gives you the time to do it. He also gives you the resources you need.

Many of us become lazy and we will procrastinate. We will come up with all kinds of excuses. Going forward, you must make up your mind that you are going to start working on the things that God places in your spirit to do for your family, your job, your church, etc.

SEPTEMBER 14

GET READY FOR GREATNESS

For this end also did I write, that I might know the proof of you, whether ye be obedient in all things

1 Corinthians 2:9

You are at the brink of something happening extraordinary in your life. You are about to experience a great move of God. Get ready! Get ready! Get ready! You have been praying, hoping, fasting, and believing and it is about to manifest. It is going to blow your mind.

You have to come to a place in your life where you have to trust God even more. You have to stand on His promises. You have to move your feet from sin. You can go ahead and praise God for what is about to happen in your life. Today, you are one step closer to your breakthrough.

SEPTEMBER 15

LEAD WITH RIGHTEOUS AUTHORITY

When the righteous are in authority, the people rejoice...

Proverbs 29:2

If you are a leader, then you must have the love of God in you in order to lead people in a righteous manner. The Word of God tells us that the people rejoice when the righteous are in authority. Would you say that you are a righteous leader in your home, on your job, in your church, in your community?

If you find that you have been slacking in this area, I want to encourage you that you can make a difference going forward. You must re-evaluate your life in order to locate if there are any problems with your leadership ability. Your goal should be to make people happy about following you. When people are sad under your leadership, then there is an indication that you may not be leading in righteous authority.

SEPTEMBER 16

LAY PROSTRATE BEFORE THE LORD

Hear, O Lord, when I cry with my voice: Have mercy also upon me, and answer me.

Psalm 27:7

Sometimes you have to just lay flat on your face and pour your heart out to God. The Bible says that Hannah poured her heart out to God. She needed and wanted something from God. She knew that He had everything that she longed for.

Today, you have to find a secret place to just go before God in serious prayer. You can stretch out before our Lord and Savior. There is always a great need to do this. You don't have to move on someone else's clock when you need something so badly from God.

SEPTEMBER 17

SAY HALELUJAH WITH A LOUD VOICE

Lord, hear my voice: let thine ears be attentive to the voice...

Psalm 130:2

Have you ever been to a sporting event, a concert, or some other event and left there hoarse? If so, the reason that happened was because you were probably yelling to the top of your lungs. Well, why is it that when you are in a church setting where the praises are going up to God, you barely open your mouth?

Many of you know that hallelujah is the highest praise that we can give to our Heavenly Father, so you should go hoarse praising Him. Can you even imagine how He feels when we show Him this kind of honor? You are only setting yourself up for the biggest blessing you can ever desire.

SEPTEMBER 18

SAY GOODBYE TO MISERY

Make haste, O God, to deliver me, make haste to help me, O Lord.

Psalm 70:1

If you have been miserable lately, you have probably not felt good. You may have been faced with some things that produce misery in your life, but you cannot stay in that place. You should never get comfortable with misery.

Have you ever noticed someone who was miserable? It seems as they wanted everyone to be in their circle and throw a "pity party" with them, right? I am certain that you told yourself, "I will not allow him or her to bring me down." Child of God, it is time to say goodbye to misery. You need to replace misery with the joy of the Lord.

SEPTEMBER 19

EAT OFF GOD'S MENU

But the fruit of the spirit is love, joy, peace, longsuffering, gentleness, goodness, faith...

Galatians 5:22

There are many food items that we eat everyday to satisfy our fleshly cravings. We go to some of the fanciest restaurants and spend a lot of money to make sure we purchase what we want. While the human body needs to be nurtured with healthy food, you must understand that your spirit has to be fed as well.

Today, you can start eating off God's menu so that you can lead a productive life and be satisfied for all the days of your life. His menu consist of peace, joy, wisdom, understanding, knowledge, strength, power, discernment, and so many other spiritual things that are needed to survive during the troubled times on your journey in life.

SEPTEMBER 20

IF YOU FALL, JUST GET BACK UP

For a just man falleth seven times, and riseth up again...

Proverbs 24:16

There are times in life when you are going to fall short of God's glory. All of us are the devil's prey, and what he wants to do is tempt us to get out of line as children of God. Our adversary gets great pleasure out of our failures and shortcomings.

You may very well yield to your flesh and fall at times, but one thing to remember is that you cannot stay down; you can "get back up again." You serve an awesome God, and you have work to do which is why you must find strength to get back to the place where you once were with God. He longs to have a relationship with you. Can't you hear Him calling your name? He doesn't want you to stay in your mess. He wants you to come out of your mess, and you can do that today.

SEPTEMBER 21

YOU SHALL WIN THE BATTLE

And I say unto thee...the gates of hell shall not prevail against it.

Matthew 16:18

If you are one of those people who feel that you are in a battle seemingly every day, I want to encourage you to keep on fighting because you are approaching the end of the battle. Although it may seem like you are going through hell, it is in the battle where you will find that you are a stronger soldier of the Lord.

You can have confidence in knowing that you have already won the battle. I want you to know that anytime you face a battle you are not fighting alone. God is in front of you, in the back of you, and on both sides of you. Although the devil may throw his best fiery darts your way, if you look at how far you have come in life, you will realize none of his darts have been able to take you out. I guarantee you will always win with God on your side.

SEPTEMBER 22

A DESIRE FOR CHANGE

Create in me a clean heart, O God; and renew a right spirit within me.

Psalm 51:10

At some point in life we all should have a desire for change. When you can remember how you used to be and how you are now, you would probably just want to have a praise party all by yourself. What is amazing is that people can tell when you have really changed. I've had many people tell me, "You are not the same. There is something different about you." I gladly respond, "Who I am now is all by the grace of God."

I know that I could not have made it this far without God, and I am certain that you realize you did not get to this point in your life without having a touch from God. Today, I want to share that you can experience change if you have a sincere desire in your heart. I have heard many people say, "God knows my heart." Yes, and He does know all of His beloved children inside and out. He knows when each of us has a desire for change for real. I encourage you today to let go of anything that is hindering you and ask God to change your ways.

SEPTEMBER 23

BE DETERMINED

For the word of the Lord is right...

Psalm 33:4

You have to be very determined when you are trying to aim toward righteousness. You will have things that will try to pull you in a different direction. You may find yourself doing and saying things that are contrary to the Word of God.

There has to be determination deep within in order for you to do what is right. On a day to day basis things are going to come against you. You are going to have thoughts that are not pure. You are going to feel like giving up. There are many other things that you are going to encounter. All and all, you have to be determined to live a life that is pleasing unto God.

SEPTEMBER 24

MAKE AN ATTEMPT

Withhold not good from them to whom it is due, when it is in the power of thine hand to do it.

Proverbs 3:27

You have to make an attempt to do something in order to see the results that you are expecting. Some of you look at things in life, and you automatically rule out the fact that you can do all things through Jesus Christ who strengthens you (Philippians 4:13). According to that scripture, you can do all...that means anything you set your heart to do.

Today, I want to encourage you to make an attempt to get the job done. Let go of every excuse that is in the back of your mind. Eliminate the "I can't" do this or that. You must have confidence in order to get anything done in life. Stop being your worst critic and make the initial steps to take care of business.

SEPTEMBER 25

GOD WILL RESTORE

Restore unto me the joy of thy salvation...

Psalm 51:12

Child of God, we all go through things in life, and some things that we face will cause us to lose our joy, peace, and happiness. Some of us can become so weak while going through certain trials and tribulations. Some of us can become so discouraged by the actions of someone else. Some of us can become so distressed when things are not seemingly lining up for us.

If you have recently gone through something that caused you to lose anything, I want you to know that God is getting ready to restore. You can come out of that place of sadness and know who your God is. Don't let anyone tell you that God won't give you back "double for your trouble."

SEPTEMBER 26

DON'T BE LAZY

I will render to a man according to his work...

Proverbs 24:29

If you are a lazy individual you will not have the drive to get anything done. Well, you probably won't do it right. The devil surely loves lazy people. He knows that if you are only going to do the bare minimum, you wouldn't dare do the things you need to do for God. You really need to get those things done around the house that you have been putting off.

If you need to mop the dirty kitchen floor, then don't put if off another day. If you need to do the laundry that is piled high, go ahead and get it done. If you are going to meet with your child's teacher because his or her grades are bad, then go ahead and setup the teacher's conference. Don't keep procrastinating as these things are important. When you fail to do these kinds of things you are operating in the spirit of laziness. And you certainly would be lazy when doing things for God, too.

SEPTEMBER 27

GOD QUICKENED MY SPIRIT

...Quicken me according to thy word.

Psalm 119:25

Child of God, we must make every attempt to live by the Word of God daily. In order to live by the Word, you have to read it. You will have a better understanding when you come to a place of doing wrong of how His Word will quicken your spirit. Yes, this happens when any of us get out of line.

You don't want to contaminate your spirit with gossip, confusion, anger or anything else; therefore, today you have an opportunity to turn from doing these evil things. When any of us succumb to these ungodly acts, God will always quicken our spirit. We have to thank Him for being such a good God and for having enough love to point us back in the right direction when we are adamant about doing these things that are not pleasing unto Him.

SEPTEMBER 28

DO YOUR BEST

The Lord will perfect that which concerneth me...

Psalm 138:8

No matter what you will ever embark on in life, make sure you always do your best. You must get this in your mind. There has been something at work, at home, at church that you have been working on, and you have not been doing a good job at all. Just think about it. God will remind you of that something.

The good thing is that He reminds us of things so that we can do better. You have to learn that He is a God of excellence, and He will reward you accordingly. Don't ever think that you are just doing it for you—you are doing it for God, too.

SEPTEMBER 29

ONE DOOR CLOSED; ONE DOOR OPEN

So he shall open, and none shall shut; and he shall shut, and none shall open.

Isaiah 22:22

Child of God, there will always be opened and closed doors. One thing to remember is that God opens and closes the doors in our lives. Today, you don't have to beg. All you have to do is "ask and it shall be given...seek and you shall find...knock and the door will be open." After you have done these things, just have FAITH, be patient and allow God to do His part.

God will always direct your path. Once He opens the door He will guide you into it. If you ever come to a place where the doors seem to be closing, just know that God is doing that for a reason. Remember, He can see beyond what we can see; He knows all things. Just trust where He leads you.

SEPTEMBER 30

CALM DOWN

Be not hasty in thy spirit to be angry: for anger resteth in the bosom of fools.

Ecclesiastes 7:9

Don't be uptight today. You need to calm down. Everything is not bad; therefore, everything should not get on your nerve. It is never that bad for you to just continue to react in an ungodly fashion. At some point you have to take full control of your temper. Stop letting it rule you!

Once you approach things in a calm manner, you will start feeling the release of tension and anger. I can tell you that it is one of the greatest feelings you can ever experience. I used to get uptight about some of the smallest things. When people would do things intentionally that got on my nerves, I would respond angrily. And it wasn't until I started responding in a calm manner, that I started feeling better. You can do the same.

OCTOBER 1

IT IS PREDESTINED

For whom he did foreknow, he also did predestinate...

Romans 8:29

You may have heard someone say, "It was predestined to happen..." We have to understand that God does predestined things to happen in our lives at His appointed time. There are a number of things that you may have prayed about, had a dream or a vision about, and it came to past. For example, you may have had an encounter with someone that you prayed years ago that you would come in contact with. Now, some people may say that it was dejavu. I would simply say that it was destined by God to happen. God divinely connects us to people, even before we ever meet them. It works the same with any other matter in life.

OCTOBER 2

DON'T BE PICKY

A little that a righteous man hath is better than the riches of many wicked.

Psalm 37:16

Some of us are way too picky. We need to stop having this picky frame of mind. If you have been praying for God to send you a spouse, bless you with a job, a car, a house, or any number of things, you need not to be so picky when He presents it to you. Having a pick mentality will cause you to miss what you have been praying for.

Remember, everything we pray for does not always appear the way we want it; it will only appear the way God wants it, so we must learn to accept it. He will always give us what we need for His glory. You better believe that it will be His best; therefore, you have to be thankful.

OCTOBER 3

HAVE COURAGE

Be of good courage, and he shall strengthen your heart...

Psalm 27:14

When you have courage there will be no option of giving up. If you surround yourself with people who don't want to progress or are used to giving up, you will most likely lose focus and tell yourself, "I am just going to give up." There is no point of going on."

I challenge you today to keep going. You may have come to a place where you want to embark on something new, and you need the courage to follow through because the task may seem a bit difficult. Well, this is just what you will need. You should only focus on the outcome. Just know that God will give you the strength to do what He plants in your mind and heart to do. I say to you, "Have courage."

OCTOBER 4

THE FAVOR OF GOD

A good man obtaineth favor of the Lord...

Proverbs 12:2

When you have the favor of God, you will no doubt get things that some people have been longing to get for years. The favor of God will open the door for the extraordinary things. The favor of God will make you excel far beyond your imagination. The favor of God will shake some things loose. The favor of God is awesome.

Today, you can decree that the favor of God is upon your life. The Word of God says, "Decree a thing and it shall be established unto thee..." This in and of itself is powerful. Therefore, going forward all you have to do is DECREE that it be so. You are so deserving of His favor.

OCTOBER 5

DEPRESSION HAS TO LEAVE YOU

Bring my soul out of prison...

Psalm 142:7

Child of God, the enemy will whisper all manner of negative things in your ear. These things will only make you depressed. If you experience depression for a long period of time, you will find yourself in a cave. You will feel like you are confined as a prisoner. You will throw temper tantrums in this cave. You will throw pity parties in this cave. You will seemingly only attract depressed people, circumstances and situations in your cave. You must realize that you cannot find peace in a cave of depression. I have a question for you: Are you ready to come out of the cave of depression?

If you have answered "yes," then you can surely come out today. You can no longer allow depression to have dominion over you. Whatever is causing you to experience depression year after year, it is time for you to reign. You must tell yourself, "I will no longer be depressed."

OCTOBER 6

TAKE YOUR HANDS OFF THE SITUATION

The Lord is my shepherd...

Psalm 23:1

Child of God, many of us will try to do only what God can do. It is time to trust Him with everything that you have been dealing with. You have been trying to fix that situation way too long. Has anything changed? Aren't you just tired of trying to do it on your own? Are you ready to just take your hands off the situation?

Once you relinquish whatever that situation is to God, you will feel so much better. I want to encourage you today to release it. You have messed it up when you tried to fix it. I guarantee when you give it to God for real, you will see immediate results in your favor.

OCTOBER 7

DON'T BE A PRETENDER; BE REAL

The wicked watcheth the righteous...

Psalm 37:32

There is no need for you to be a pretender. I once heard a pastor say, "You can only pretend for so long. The real you will soon come out." If you really give thought to that statement, you will probably agree that it is true. God knows when each of us is pretending, and He knows when we are real. If you notice that when people are misleading and big pretenders, they will always try to hide who they really are.

They pretend until they get what they want. If you really think about it, you will say that is totally the character of Satan. He appears to show himself to be real, but He only pretends until He draws you in. Once he does that, he uses you to the fullest and then devours you. Likewise, when people are real from the beginning, you would agree that they are operating with godly character. Do you know why? It is because "Jesus is real."

OCTOBER 8

NO MORE SELF-PITY

My soul, wait thou only upon God; for my expectation is from him.

Psalm 62:5

It is the dawn of a new day. You have to snap back into reality. It is time to hold your head up. You have to speak to your situation. God has equipped you with everything you need to survive, and He is right in the fight with you. Yes, you may be down and out right now, but you still have the breath of life to make things happen. Don't you know that this is the day the Lord has made?

It is time for you to rejoice and speak to whatever mountain is in your life. With your faith, it has to move. That storm has to cease right now in the name of Jesus Christ. I want you to know that there is joy on the other side of your storm. There is a blessing on the other side of that mountain. There is peace in your crisis. It is time out for self-pity.

OCTOBER 9

DON'T BE DECEIVED

Let no man deceive you by any means...

2 Thessalonians 2:3

Child of God, we are living in a time where a lot of people are being deceived. You have to be very careful that you don't become a victim of the enemy's snare. Remember, our adversary will use anything or anyone. He wants to catch you off guard. He uses people every day who want to gain something, and they will scam or lie to get what they want. They don't care who is affected by their actions. They are simply "workers for Satan." Starting today, I want to encourage you to be careful that you don't fall into the enemy's deception trap.

OCTOBER 10

GOD IS HOPE

Now the God of hope will fill you with all joy and peace...

Romans 15:13

You may have been hoping for something that you know only God can do. He will fill you with all that you have hoped for—a change, a blessing, a promotion, joy, peace, a spouse or something else. He will fill you with those natural and spiritual things. It is His desire to give you what you hope and ask for. He is an unselfish God. Today, I want to encourage you to keep your hope in God and don't look outside of Him for anything else.

OCTOBER 11

GOD IS WITH YOU IN THE FIERY FURNANCE

...I see four men loose walking in the midst of the fire, and they have no hurt; and the form of the fourth is like the Son of God.

Daniel 3:25

You may feel like you have been thrown in the fiery furnace by your family members, so-called friends, co-workers, and some of your church members. You have realized that you have a real enemy. There are times in life when you will behold the jealous, backbiting, evil, cold-hearted people plotting against you, talking about you, and digging ditches for you. Yes, God will allow you to see exactly what they are doing.

If you feel like you are in a fiery furnace today, I want to encourage you that you are not in it alone—God is with you just as He was in it with Shadrach, Meshach and Abednego (Read more in Daniel, Chapter 3). Therefore, don't focus on those who have thrown you in the fiery furnace, just know that you will come out as gold because "What don't break you will certainly make you." You will soon be able to look your enemy in the face and say, "You meant it for my bad, but God meant it for my good."

OCTOBER 12

THE STUMBLINGBLOCK

Refrain thy foot from their path...

Proverbs 1:15

There will always be stumbling blocks in your way, especially when you are traveling down the path that God has you on. But, it is okay. These stumbling blocks are there to make you "stumble" on your journey, and sometimes they can make the best of us quit. When you know that you are going in the right direction, you cannot allow anything to get you off course.

Today, you may notice a stumbling block, and it is not going to magically move. You must take charge and jump over it, go around it, or just move it. God has given you the power you need to do either one of those things. One thing to remember is that people can serve as a stumbling block in your life. Be very watchful and listen to God's voice concerning people who are in your life and those who are eager to be a part of your life.

OCTOBER 13

FAITHFULNESS IS REWARDING

...Thy faithfulness reached unto the clouds.

Psalm 36:5

Child of God, you have made many sacrifices, and I want you to know that God has seen everyone that you have made. Your faithfulness has reached Heaven. You have been faithful in your ministry, in your home, on your job, and with everything else. Don't you know that God loves when any of us just stick with something?

You have shown him how much you honor Him through your faithfulness. You have not given up on the task that He has instructed you to do. You have done your best with what you have had to work with. Your faithfulness is going to bring many rewards. Today, I want you to turn up the expectancy notch. Your reward will be great.

OCTOBER 14

PERSISTENCE WILL PAY OFF

And let us not be weary in well doing: for in due season we shall reap, if we faint not.

Galatians 6:9

You may have been very persistent in the things of God, and I want you to know that God sees you. You may have had people to discount everything that you have done. I want to tell you that you no longer have to be concerned with being validated by anyone. You don't have to entertain those people who continues to say things like, "It doesn't take all that. You need to slow your role. You are just doing too much." These things will make you take your eyes off the mission. I want to encourage you to rest assure that your persistence will pay off.

OCTOBER 15

YOU HAVE COME TOO FAR

Though thy beginning was small, yet thy latter end should greatly increase.

Psalm 8:7

Child of God, be encouraged today. Keep pushing forward in whatever God has purposed you to do. You are no longer at the starting point of your assignment. You have come too far on your journey. If you are having thoughts of giving up because you can't see in the natural realm all the things that God is doing behind the scene, you need to immediately cast down those thoughts.

I want to share that you have to be in the spirit in order to discern what God is doing spiritually in your life. Our natural mind and flesh can never conceive this. Just keep the faith. When you have faith in Him, it will give you the confidence in knowing that "God didn't bring you this far to leave you."

OCTOBER 16

RISE UP

...Rise up early in the morning, and stand before...

Exodus 8:20

Child of God, don't ever think that is okay for you to stay down, because you can rise up today! Rise up, men! Rise up, ladies! Rise up, children! God has made this beautiful day and we must rise up and rejoice. Just because you have had some tough times this year, does not mean it is over for you. You can declare that the enemy will not win.

The season has just changed in your life, and you have a lot to look forward to. You must speak into existence what you need. You can claim what you have already prayed to God for. You should thank Him for moving you in a new direction in this season of your life. Go ahead and trust God for the blessings that He is about to pour out to you. Step on the devil's head and tell him that he is already defeated! Run and shout like never before! Rise up with power, knowing that God is on your side!

OCTOBER 17

JUST CAN'T MAKE IT WITHOUT GOD

If it had not been the Lord who was on our side...

Psalm 124:1

Do you think that it is possible to make it without God? I hope that your answer is "No." If anyone thinks that they can make it without God, then it is evident that they are a nonbeliever. We all need God every day of the year, and every step of the way. It is absolutely impossible to make it without our Heavenly Father. I can guarantee that He will be by your side when everyone else turns their back on you.

We have to depend on Him for shelter, food, clothing, and everything else. We need Him for peace, joy, happiness, etc. He is a supplier of all the natural and spiritual things that we all need to make it on our journey. You should always want to be in His presence.

OCTOBER 18

IT WILL WORK

Be strong...and work: for I am with you, saith the Lord of host.

Haggai 2:4

You have to believe that whatever you put your mind to, it will work. If you are a person who is operating under the spirit of doubt, you need to let it go today. You have to know without any form of doubt that what you are set out to do in this life, it will work.

Remember, God didn't say in His Word that you can do some things through Jesus Christ; He profoundly said that we as believers can do "All things through Christ Jesus..." You need to stop being afraid of what people can or cannot do to you. You are God's child who has work to do in the vineyard, and you must realize that everything will work out for you. Go ahead and use that inner strength to do whatever it takes to get the job done.

OCTOBER 19

GOD WILL STRENGTHEN YOU

The Lord will give strength unto his people...

Psalm 29:11

There is nothing like it when God strengthens you. His power cannot be compared to anything else. If you have been battling with something that you have felt has had a stronghold on your life, then I serve as a living witness that God will give you that much needed strength to "shake that devil off." That is exactly what you are up against, a demon from the pits of hell.

He brings the chaos in our lives to weaken our faith, our joy, and everything else. His attacks literally will break you down. But all it takes is the power of God to break every yoke, every stronghold, and every force. Today, I guarantee that you can depend and stand on the strength of God.

OCTOBER 20

DON'T BE 'CARE-FREE'

...Members should have the same care one for another.

1 Corinthians 12:25

There are many people among us who don't have a care at all. They don't care if you are hurting. They don't care if you are sick. They don't care if you have a need. You have to make sure that you are not in this category. If you have had an encounter in life that has made you have the "care-free" mentality, I want to encourage you get free today. Don't let those bad experiences cause you to be "care-free" and full of anger and strife.

You don't ever want your blessings to stop because of this kind of mindset. You must remember that God cares about all of us. This is certainly why He gave His Son for us. Therefore, we should have a caring spirit like Jesus Christ. Being in the body of Christ, it is a requirement that we care for one another.

OCTOBER 21

A RIGHTEOUS CRY

*The righteous cry and the Lord heareth, and delivered them out of
all their troubles.*

Psalm 34:17

God knows that His people are going to cry at times. Guess
what? He hears the cry of the righteous. You may have been
enduring a whole lot of pain. You have been hurt many
times. You have been criticized and judged over and over
again. Your heart is even aching right now. He knows that
you have been overwhelmed.

Child of God, let me tell you something. He is about to do
something in your life that you never thought he would do.
Hold on! He is turning it around as you sit there with your
head held down. Your righteous does count in God's book,
and so does your cry. The Lord hears it, and he will deliver
you on this day.

OCTOBER 22

NO NEED TO BE JEALOUS

For jealousy is the rage of a man....

Proverbs 6:34

There is no need for any of us as children of God to be jealous of each other. Today, just think of the reasons that you are jealous of someone else. You want to then ask God to help you with your confidence level so that you won't feel the need to be jealous of anyone. You will find that jealousy produces anger and hatred. I am certain that you have heard "What God does for one; He can do for the other." Go ahead and latch on to this truth. This is something that you need to get deep in your spirit today.

OCTOBER 23

PRESS ON ANYWAY

...The people pressed upon him to hear the Word of God...

Luke 5:1

If you feel like pressing on, just say, "I have a press in my spirit today?" Someone may have told you that there is no point of you doing that because you see it is not working out for you. They may have called you a fool. They may have called you crazy. There is no telling what else they may have called you.

You have to remember that everything will work out for your good, regardless. You don't have a "quit" in your spirit. You have a "press" in your spirit, and that is what God really looks at. So, I encourage you to press on anyway because what you are pressing toward is not too far out of your reach.

OCTOBER 24

JUST SAY YES LORD

Grace be unto you...from our Lord Jesus Christ who have himself for our sins that he might deliver us from this present evil world, according to the will of God...

Galatians 1:3-4

If you have been saying, "God, I am just tired of this and that. I can't take it anymore. What is the purpose of going on?" Are you ready to change some of the words you use daily? Well, this is your day. I encourage you to start saying, "Yes, Lord!"

Remember, there is nothing too hard for Him. You are right where He wants you to be. It is all a part of your growth process. Through your toughest trials and tribulations, God is developing a new person that He can use for His glory.

OCTOBER 25

LAZINESS PRODUCES NEGATIVE RESULTS

...Where there is no vision, the people perish.

Proverbs 29:18

Are you ready to get up in do something today? Are you ready to make things happen? If you answered "Yes" to these questions, I want you to know that you are getting ready to be delivered from laziness. This kind of spirit will cause life to pass you by. You will be looking at everyone around you succeeding, and you will be wondering why you are not moving.

You must realize that you cannot do much with the spirit of laziness. If you have a vision, you have to do something to ensure that you fulfill it. I will tell you that the spirit of laziness is one of your biggest enemies. You have to tell that spirit that you have no more room for it in your life, and that it has to go right now.

OCTOBER 26

BE UNIFIED NOT DIVIDED

Behold, how good and how pleasant it is for brethren (and sisters) to dwell together in unity.

Psalm 133:1

There are so many of us Christians who are divided. We have allowed our adversary to cause such a great division among us. It is time for us to be unified in the name of Jesus Christ. Do you know that God loves unity? He wants us to be unified in our families, in our churches and in our communities.

We must come together and trample the devil. We can no longer give him room to cause division. Today, I encourage you get on one accord and make it right with whoever you have a problem with. Don't let this keep you from walking in unity. I am certain you have heard, "Together we stand, divided we fall."

OCTOBER 27

DESIRE TO DO WHAT IS RIGHT

Let integrity and uprightness preserve me...

Psalm 25:21

When you desire to do what is right according to the Word of God, you will find yourself doing right. I want you to know that God is always there to direct your path when you just think about pleasing Him. If you have been practicing wrongdoing, you can start doing what is right. The choice to do right should always be the option you make, regarding any situation. All you have to do is make a sound decision not to do wrong.

OCTOBER 28

TOLERATE JESUS NOT THE DEVIL

Jesus Christ the same yesterday, and today, and forever.

Hebrews 13:8

We Christians should never get tired of Jesus. He is always the same; he never changes. We are an extension of Him. We must tolerate Him 24 hours a day for He is the One who gives us everything we need from day to day. He is the One who will never leave our side. He tolerates us because He loves us.

We can never allow the devil to come between us and God. We should never tolerate him or his evil doings. The devil appears to be light just to lure you in, but you will find out that he is here on earth to devour the children of God. I encourage you to stand up to the devil today and let him know that he is a loser, a thief, and a liar. You have to tell him that you will no longer let him rule your life; that you have tolerated him and his mess long enough.

OCTOBER 29

YOUR TESTIMONY IS ENCOURAGING

They overcame him by the blood of the Lamb, and the word of their testimony...

Revelation 12:11

Do you have a testimony? If so, you should share it with others. Someone needs to be encouraged, and it is in the words of your testimony. Someone is experiencing sickness and they need to hear about how God healed your body. Someone is experiencing financial hardship and they need to hear how God blessed you with an overflow.

Someone just loss their job and they need to hear how God still provided when you were unemployed. Someone is experiencing marital problems and they need to hear how God mended your marriage. There are people all across this globe that is facing something, and your testimony can help them.

OCTOBER 30

IT IS SO ACCORDING TO YOUR FAITH

...According to your faith be it unto you.

Matthew 9:29

As a child of God, you must operate with faith in Him. The Word basically tells us that it is so. Therefore, whatever you have been petitioning God for is getting ready to come forth. It has to manifest. It is possible all because of your faith. I want to encourage you today to keep the faith. Don't let anything or anyone cause you to doubt or waver. You have to believe and call God to His Word—Lord, you said, "...Be it unto you (me)."

OCTOBER 31

LORD, I WILL GO

I will go in the strength of the Lord God...

Psalm 71:16

When you are committed and sold out to God, it will be impossible for you to reject executing your purpose. Your purpose requires for you to be ready at all times. You won't have to worry about it being a tug-a-war when you have been sent by God to do or say something. Your spirit will say, "Yes, Lord," because you have full confidence and faith that God has equipped you for the task at hand.

You will be willing to come out of your comfort zone in order to go forth. Today, I want to encourage those of you who have had fear in going forward to put on your warfare clothes and be ready to go when you hear that still small voice say, "Your purpose is at hand and it is time to go..."

NOVEMBER 1

USE THE POWER GOD GAVE YOU

Now unto him that is able to do exceeding, abundantly above all that we ask or think, according to the power that worketh in us.

Ephesians 3:20

Child of God, you have so much power that God has given you. When you don't use it when needed, you can be overtaken. To be perfectly honest, we Christian need power everyday to fight against our adversary.

So today, if you feel the need to cuss somebody out on your job, you can use the power to bridle your tongue. If you have an urge to eat everything that is in your view, you can use the power to fast. When you feel the need to lie, you can use the power to tell the truth; knowing that God is all truth. When you feel the need to do anything that is contrary to God's will, you can use the power God has given you to stick with the Word.

NOVEMBER 2

MOVE OUT THE WAY AND DO IT GOD'S WAY

If a man loves me (Jesus), he will keep my words...

Matthew 14:23

You have to learn to move out of the way and do it God's way. Have you noticed that some of the things that you have been trying to do are at a standstill? It could very well be because you are too adamant about doing it your way. The task that God gave you is not about you at all.

God really wants to work it out for you. He wants everything that He has purposed for you to do to glorify Him. You have to get out of the way and tune in to what He is instructing you to do and leading you to go. As you move forward, you should learn to do it God's way.

NOVEMBER 3

GOD WILL PERSERVE YOU

Preserve my soul; for I am holy...

Psalm 86:2

I want you to know that God will preserve you. I am certain there have been some things that you wanted to do, and you know they were not right. Some of you have been trying to steer away from the sins of this world, and you have made a commitment that you will do right. Good sees your heart and He knows that your spirit has been reaching out to Him.

It is an honor when you know that you cannot do anything within your power; therefore, you submit your will to His because you know that you need Him to step in and help you. I want to tell you that He has stepped in.

NOVEMBER 4

HAVE A HOLY GHOST PARTY NOT A PITY PARTY

...The Holy Ghost shall come upon thee, and the power of the Highest shall overshadow thee...

Luke 1:35

Child of God, the Holy Ghost shall come upon you; therefore, you have to be mindful of what kind of party you are going to have for yourself once you have this experience. You should never want to throw a "pity party." God is looking for those of us who will have a "Holy Ghost party," because this kind of party makes Him pour continued blessings upon us.

When you are having this kind of party you are not even concerned about others joining you; it is the kind of party that only requires you. When you have this kind of party it also means that you are worshipping, praising and honoring God all at the same time. Keep having your "Holy Ghost" party! I guarantee you will feel good after you have finished.

NOVEMBER 5

YOUR SINS ARE FORGIVEN

...Your sins are forgiven you for his name's sake.

1 John 2:12

God forgives each of us for our sins; therefore, don't let anyone hold anything over your head. Think about it: If God does not hold anything over your head, why should anyone else do such thing? I encourage you today to come out of condemnation and know that Almighty God is your keeper. Always remember that you have to forgive those who trespass against you, who talk about you, who mistreat you, and do anything that will cause harm to you.

NOVEMBER 6

THE BLESSING HAS YOUR FULL NAME ON IT

And give thee the blessing of Abraham...

Genesis 28:4

God is confirming this day that He is about to release an overflow of His blessings upon the people of God. Guess what? All the blessings he has for you have your full name written on them; therefore, you can enjoy what is about to happen in your life. You can go ahead and shout about it. You have been obedient. You have been patient. You have been faithful. You have been prayerful. You have been a blessing to others, and now it is your time to receive the blessing that has your full name on it. Receive it today!

NOVEMBER 7

DON'T BE HAUGHTY

Pride goeth before destruction and a haughty spirit before a fall.

Proverbs 16:18

Many of us come to a place of haughtiness. I can assure you on today that no one (I mean, no one) is above God. Therefore, we all have to come to a place of submission. We have to submit to our Heavenly Father and obey His will.

When you are haughty, you are basically setting yourself up for a hard fall. Being haughty is just like being arrogant (and proud), and we know that God does not rejoice off our arrogance. We must always remember that we need God, and He does not need us. If you are guilty of being haughty, I want to encourage you to ask God to help you. Take the back seat and let God be the driver of your life!

NOVEMBER 8

LET GO OF THE MESS

Many are the afflictions of the righteous; but the Lord delivereth him out of them all.

Psalm 34:19

Aren't you tired of your mess? There should come a time when you should just get completely tired of your mess. Once you have identified your mess, you must ask God to pull you out and give you the strength not to return. Interestingly, when God brings some us out of a situation, many of us will go back again and again. You have to speak to your mess, declaring "No More." I challenge you to do it today. I also encourage you to focus your attention on "bigger and better" things, not on the things that will lead to mess.

NOVEMBER 9

GOD IS CONNECTING

Samuel also said unto Saul, the Lord sent me to anoint thee to be king over his people...

1 Samuel 15:1

Child of God, you may be longing to connect with the right people—those who are going to be instrumental to your growth, your success, your blessings, etc. You are in the preparation stage now, and God is going to bless you to cross the path of those people. In turn, you are going to be the person they need to connect with as well. I encourage you to set your heart and mind on connection—a business partner, a marriage partner, a fruitful friendship, a ministry partner...is coming your way. I once heard a preacher say, "It's connection time." Can you receive that today?

NOVEMBER 10

DON'T BE UNSTABLE

A double minded man is unstable in all his ways.

James 1:8

Each of us has to have stability in our life. When you are a stable person, it helps you to maintain in every area of your life. It is quite difficult for any of us to move forward when we are unstable. When you are stable though you are giving God room to come in and make your situation better. You are not going back and forth. You will make a commitment to stay right where you are until God moves you. You will submit your mind to God; therefore, you won't even have room to waver.

Some of you have told yourselves that it is God's way or no way. You have realized the importance of it no longer being your way, and that is because you have stability in your life. For those of you who are struggling in this area, I encourage you to relinquish your thoughts to God so that He can give you stability. Stop trying to do things on your on! Many of you may know by now that we can all make a big mess when doing things our way.

NOVEMBER 11

IT HAS BEEN LOOSED IN HEAVEN

...whatsoever thou shalt bind on earth shall be bound in heaven: and whatsoever thou shalt loose on earth shall be loosed in heaven.

Matthew 16:19

As you start your day praying, you must have faith and confidence that whatever you bind on earth, it will be loosed in heaven. If you are not going to believe that it will be loosed in heaven, then you should not even bind it. You will probably find yourself having to bind certain things daily.

If you wake up with a headache, then you know that sickness is trying to creep up on you, so you began to bind the pain that results from this headache and call God to His Word, confessing that you are made whole. If you wake up with bills on your mind, you have to bind the spirit of worry, speaking that God is your provider. Whatever it is that is not consistent with the Word of God, you need to bind so that it can be released in Heaven. Remember, God is your Heavenly Father. Therefore, call out the things that you want to be loosed and just get ready for it to be released from Heaven.

NOVEMBER 12

SUPPORT SOMEONE'S GOOD EFFORTS

...And they beckoned unto their partners...that they should come and help them.

Luke 5:7

There are many people in this world who are doing wonderful things, and you can help them with the resources that God has given you to support their good efforts, especially those who are doing work for the Kingdom of God. One thing to remember is that God has blessed you so that you can extend those blessings to others. I want to encourage you this day to not hold on to everything—release some of it, and keep your hands open to receive more from the ONE who provides.

NOVEMBER 13

EMAIL OR TEXT SOMEONE A POSTIVE MESSAGE

I delight to do thy will, O my God...

Psalm 40:8

Child of God, there are so many people in the world today who own a cell phone or have access to a computer. With this being said, you have a brand new opportunity to share a kind word without calling someone. You can simply send them an email or a text message. That is so amazing! It is a blessing that technology has evolved to a point to where we can use it to glorify God or glorify the devil.

I encourage you today to glorify God by sending a positive message to someone through an email or by a text message. That person will be happy you did. Most importantly, God will be pleased with your actions.

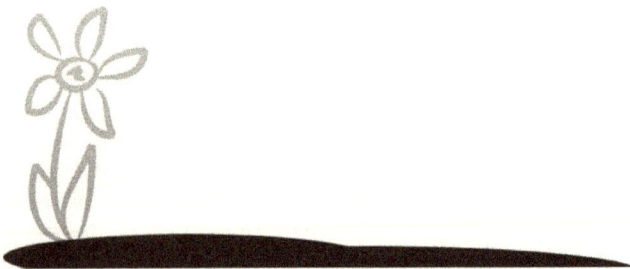

NOVEMBER 14

GREAT THINGS ARE HAPPENING IN THE ATMOSPHERE

...Who is so great a God as our God?

Psalm 77:13

Our God is great and He is always doing great things in our lives. God is about to plant a new idea in your mind to replace those thoughts of failure, fear, and the unknown. You must be careful to stay out of the presence of negative-minded people. The reason for this is that God is getting ready to shift some things in the atmosphere so you must be in position to implement and carry out the idea that He has given to you.

If you are around negative people, they will try to hinder you. These great things that are happening in the atmosphere is for those who are sincere about God and have a desire to get some things done while it is yet day. That is why He is giving you these new ideas so that He can stir up your spirit to do the work.

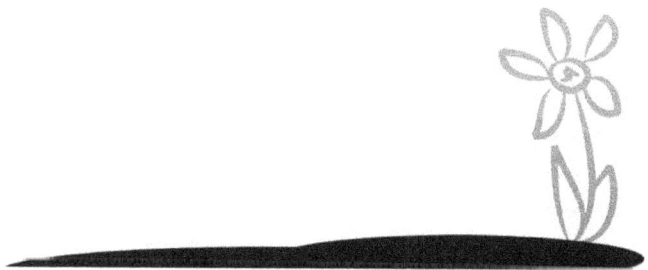

NOVEMBER 15

BE KIND

And be ye kind one to another...

Ephesians 4:32

As children of God, we are to be kind to one another. Some people are always on the edge; therefore, they feel like they can treat people any kind of way. Some people are not even kind to themselves; therefore, this has a direct impact on how they treat others. I want to encourage you today to look in the mirror and say something good about yourself. Buy yourself a nice gift. Treat yourself to lunch. Respect yourself. When you learn to treat yourself kind, you will start treating others kind. Ask God to help you as it is His will that you be kind to everyone.

NOVEMBER 16

GROWING PAINS

As new babes, desire the sincere milk of the word that ye may grow thereby.

1 Peter 2:2

All of us are going to have growing pains in our lives if we desire growth. If you haven't already experienced those kinds of pains, then they will surely come. Child of God, we are not always going to feel so good when we are going through the growth process either. Oftentimes our resistance can be associated with the "growing pains."

When we become too complacent, we are not so willing to embrace change, which is a part of the growth process. I was once there; therefore, you should accept the challenge of the starting point of your growth process. The pain will not last a long time. When you get to your next level, you won't even remember the pain that you had to endure to get you to this level. That is the beauty in going from "level to level, faith to faith, and glory to glory."

NOVEMBER 17

A REFRESHING WORD FROM GOD WILL REVIVE YOU

Though I walk in the midst of trouble, thou wilt revive me...

Psalm 138:7

There are many churches across the globe that has had tent revivals. Of course, we all know that the purpose of a revival is so that the people of God can be uplifted, rejuvenated, refreshed, and so forth. God wants to revive your heavy spirit. He sees that you have been overwhelmed, confused, anxious, and battling in your mind. I encourage you today to embrace this moment of revival that is about to take place in your life.

NOVEMBER 18

THIS IS NOT THE END FOR YOU

Though thy beginning was small, yet thy latter end should greatly increase.

Psalm 8:7

Child of God, you may be at the brink of giving up, and you just got started. Because you have come out of one trial and entering another one, does not mean that this is the end for you. You may feel that you have come to the end of the road. Don't you know that your latter end is greater than the beginning?

Don't think for a moment that God is not with you. I am certain you have had those thoughts, right? Well, I want to give you a word of encourage today to speak to your trial, declaring that it will not take you out; that you have the victory, and "It's not over until God's says it's over."

NOVEMBER 19

TO BE MEEK IS TO BE BLESSED

But the meek shall inherit the earth; and shall delight themselves in the abundance of peace.

Psalm 37:11

When you are meek, you are setting yourself up for unlimited blessings. You shall inherit the earth as the Word says. That simply means that there is nothing that you have need for that won't be supplied. God has so much in store for you. There is just something about having a spirit of meekness. This is one of Jesus' attributes, and that is why we have to love Him for all that He is in our individual lives.

NOVEMBER 20

GOD WILL FIGHT FOR YOU

....They shall fight, because the Lord is with them...

Zechariah 10:5

There are too many Christian who are trying to fight their battles in the flesh. Interestingly, some of us think we can literally win these battles while fighting in our flesh. You have to let God fight your battles. When you come under certain attacks, you can rest assure that there is a spiritual demon behind that attack. Your flesh can't beat a demon. Don't worry. I encourage you today to let God fight for you; know that He is with you.

NOVEMBER 21

TELL POVERTY GOOD-BYE

...He shall have more abundance...

Matthew 13:12

Child of God, it is not our Father's will that we live a life of financial defeat. He knows that we have financial obligations, and everything we need is provided through Him. Let us walk in obedience so that we can obtain these things and come out of lack—for good. God sees that you have freely given, and you will receive—starting today!

I want you to just make the following declarations out of your own mouth. "I am no longer broke. I have all that I need and much of what I want. I am not a fool with my money. I sow my seeds on good ground. I make sound money decisions. I will live and lead an abundant life, financially and otherwise. I am free from poverty; therefore, I am telling poverty good-bye today."

NOVEMBER 22

RELEASE ALL GRUDGES

For we are consumed by thine anger...

Psalm 90:7

There are a vast number of Christians who are holding grudges against someone—a family member, a friend, a church member, a coworker, or someone else. It is time to release it. This is not good for you. The grudges that some of you are holding against others stem from what someone said or did to you, which led to your anger. All you have to do is forgive this person (s), and move forward. Stop holding all the animosity and anger in your heart. I encourage you to let God fill your heart with love so that you can forgive.

NOVEMBER 23

DON'T BE PRESSURED

...O Lord, I am oppressed...

Isaiah 38:14

Many times in life we are pressured into doing things that we really don't want to do. If this has happened to you, I want to encourage you to not let anyone pressure you. When someone pressures you, it basically adds unnecessary stress to your life and you can become oppressed. You end up complaining because you really don't want to give into their request.

You must realize that when you are under pressure you will make high impact decisions that you will end up regretting. Going forward, make sure you don't let people pressure you into marriage, into moving to a home or an apartment that you can't afford, into taking a position that you are unhappy with, or anything else.

NOVEMBER 24

WATCH FOR SATAN'S BAIT

Behold, I give unto you power to tread on serpent...and over all the power of the enemy.

Luke 10:19

One thing you must learn is that Satan has baits, and you have to be very watchful for them. Our adversary's mission is to lure the children of God into his baits; fornication, adultery, anger, strife, hatred, jealousy are just a few of his baits. If he can get you to engage in any of those things mentioned, then his mission would be accomplished. I encourage you to watch for his baits today and be careful not to succumb to any of them. You already have the power to tread on serpents.

NOVEMBER 25

BE THANKFUL FOR WHAT YOU HAVE

...Be thankful to him, and bless his name.

Psalm 100:4

No matter what you have in your possession, you should be very thankful. It certainly could be worse. All you have to do is think about those who are less fortunate than you are. If this is what it takes for you to realize how bless you are, then you should go ahead and meditate on it.

You may not have all you want to eat today, but you have enough food to fill your stomach. You may not have a car to drive, but you do have someone close to you who don't mind taking you to where you need to go. You may not have the clothes you'd like to wear, but you do have something nice in your closet. People of God, you must learn to be grateful for what God has already done for you. You should always keep Him first in your life.

NOVEMBER 26

HAVE AN EXPERIENCE WITH GOD

...My heart had great experience...

Ecclesiastes 1:17

Do you want to have an experience with God today? You can have an experience with God like you have never had. You can have that ultimate worship experience, that Holy Ghost experience, that joy experience, and any other spiritual experience with Him. He is delighted when we desire to share those kinds of experiences with Him. I want to encourage you to stay in His presence and don't let anyone interfere with your experiences with God.

NOVEMBER 27

GOD WILL GUIDE YOU THROUGH THE FOG OF YOUR LIFE

...God is our God forever and ever: he will be our guide even unto death.

Psalm 48:14

Have you ever noticed how the fog outside early in morning makes it hard to see? When you turn on the defrost button in your vehicle, it usually makes it clear to see. There have been times when it was too foggy outside; I had to pull my car over to the side of the road until it was clear enough for me to see the road.

Child of God, I want you to know that when you have certain encounters in your life, they are just like the "fog" outside on some mornings. These encounters can make it difficult for you to see your way. Well, I am here to tell you that God is there to guide you through your fog of life. He will ensure that the "fog" does not hinder your prayer life, your praise, your worship or anything else. You have to trust Him to guide you just as you would trust the defrost functioning in your vehicle to clear your windows so that you can see the road as you are traveling from one destination to the next.

NOVEMBER 28

BE THE BEST EXAMPLE

The Lord tireth the righteous...

Psalm 11:5

There are many people you can be an example to. If you are a parent, be your child's best example. You can be an example to people on your job, at church, and even in your community. When you are a great example, people won't be reluctant to follow you.

You have to realize that God is looking for those of us who will be the best example everywhere we go. I challenge you today to look at your life and see if you are the best example. Do you think that you can do better? Always remember that if you partner with God, He will show you how to become a positive, godly example daily.

NOVEMBER 29

MY SOUL LONGS FOR GOD

My soul longeth, yea, even fainteth for the courts of the Lord: my heart and my flesh crieth out for the living God.

Psalm 84:2

Child of God, there will come a time when you feel like you are all alone. Some of you may be in this position today, and your soul is longing and crying out for God. You need to know that He is with you. You just want to hear Him speak to you because you feel like He has left you. Our Heavenly Father will not forsake any of us. I want you to be encouraged from this day forward and know that He is there to answer your cry.

NOVEMBER 30

SWITCH TO JESUS

Come ye after me (Jesus), and I will make you to become fishers of men.

Mark 1:17

Have any of you ever received something in the mail, whether it was from a cable company, your cell phone company, a college or university, or a number of other places asking you to switch to their service? When you received this document, you had to ponder if you were going to make the switch. Well, I want to present something to you today that you don't have to think about whether you want to make this switch—and I am talking about the switch to JESUS.

This is the type of switch where you don't have to ponder. This switch is very crucial for those of you who haven't made it yet, and one you won't ever regret. Some of you have been traveling in the wrong direction. Because of the position that many of you are in, it is evident that you have been on the wrong track. Some of you have forgotten about Jesus. If this is you, I want to encourage you to come from that dead position and switch to Jesus.

DECEMBER 1

TRY SOMETHING DIFFERENT

I will instruct thee and teach thee...

Psalm 32:8

Do you ever get tired of doing the same thing? If so, "I dare you to be different." If you are getting the same negative results from what you are doing, then that should warrant you to do something different. It is so easy to complain when things are not working in your favor, but all you have to do is examine your situation; you will probably find that in order to get the positive results that you are looking for, you must do something totally different. And you can start today!

DECEMBER 2

YOU ARE ROYALTY

But ye are a chosen generation, a royal priesthood, an holy nation,
a peculiar people...

1Peter 2:9

You are a royalty. God is honored to have you as His beloved daughter and son. He is excited about you being in His family. Since you are part of His family, I want you to know that you are chosen for greatness. You are covered. You will be granted your heart's desire. You will always be in His presence; that means He will protect you as long as you live. Aren't you glad to be a part of His family? Why don't you introduce the Father of your family to those who don't know Him? You can make this introduction every opportunity to you have to be a witness to your Father's goodness.

DECEMBER 3

GOT TO LOVE YOUR VALLEY EXPERIENCES

Every valley shall be exalted...

Isaiah 40:2

Child of God, we are all going to have a valley experience (s), and you can love that kind of experience. I want you to know that there is a reason for this kind of experience. It gives you the opportunity to really see who your God is. As I reflect upon the various stories in the Bible of those who had those (Daniel in the Lion's Den, David, Paul and Silas, and the list goes on) kinds of experiences, I get happy all over again just thinking about God "showing up and showing out."

If you can just latch on to the glory that was revealed behind these people's deliverance that is mentioned in the Holy Book, it will show you that we have a God that is not only in the valley with us, but ONE who will bring us out as "pure as gold.' I want to encourage you to just love right we you are, and you can have a greater love and appreciation for where you are headed.

DECEMBER 4

SEEK THE LORD

Seek ye the Lord while he may be found, call ye upon him while he is near.

Isaiah 55:6

As long as you live you will learn that Jesus can be found if you seek and have a desire to find Him. He is not far away. He is so near, but all you have to do is accept Him as your Lord and Savior. If you have already accepted Him, but have backslidden, you can just come back. His arms are always opened. He is not like that person who is angry because you left them; He is One of a "second" chance.

DECEMBER 5

BE FAITHFUL

A faithful man shall abound with blessings...

Proverbs 28:20

I challenge you today to be faithful in all that you do for the Lord. If you find yourself slacking, ask God to give you the strength to maintain. Don't let anyone distract you or tell you that you ought to be burnt out doing God's work. You just keep been faithful. I encourage you to continue praying, keep hoping, keep fasting, and keep the "faith," and you shall abound with blessings.

DECEMBER 6

LORD, I WANT MORE

More to be desired...

Psalm 19:10

Does everything around you seem to be caving in? Are you tired of the ups and downs of life? Are you simply in a place where you feel that you need more of God? If so, I want to tell you that God is on the scene of your current situation, and He wants to give you more revelation, comfort, peace, power...more of Him. During these trying times, we all need more of Jesus.

DECEMBER 7

IT'S OVER, DON'T BEAT YOURSELF UP

O keep my soul, and deliver me...

Psalm 25:20

You may have recently had one of your snap moments, frustrated moments, sad moments, or some other moment. You finally came out of having one of your "moments," and now you continue to beat yourself up. You have not only beaten yourself up, you have allowed those around you to beat you up with their negative comments. I encourage you today to meditate on some scriptures that will help you make it through this day.

DECEMBER 8

THE BRIGHTER SIDE DO EXIST

...The Lord shall be to thee an everlasting light...

Isaiah 60:19

Because of the challenges that some of you are facing, you feel like there is no hope at all! The Word tells us that God is our light, and He will be that "light" in our lives forever. With that being said, there is a brighter side to your situation. What you are going through right now is only a test. It definitely is not going to last too long. You can't focus on the dark side of your situation; you must let that light (God) within propel you to the other side of your situation so that you can have a peace of mind.

DECEMBER 9

YOU CAN FIND SECURITY IN GOD

Pull me out of the net that they laid privily for me: for thou art my strength.

Psalm 31:4

So often we try to find security in people, places and things. And some of the people you think are for you are really against you. They will set up all kinds of traps for you. They will partner with the devil to attack you. But, I am here to tell you that you can find security in God. I encourage you to run to your safety net today, and He will ensure that you are protected from every attack of your enemy.

DECEMBER 10

GET INVOLVED IN GODLY MATTERS

For we must all appear before the judgment seat of Christ; that every one may receive the things done in his body, according to that he hath done, whether it be good or bad.

2 Corinthians 5:10

It is not uncommon for some of us to ask, "what are you getting into today, tomorrow, or the weekend?"' And the reason that many of us ask this question is because we want to be entertained by something. We want to be a part of something that others are a part of. In many cases, it is ungodly matters. If this is you, I encourage you get involved in godly matters. You can find out how you can help feed the homeless, assist with a women's retreat or a men's conference, assist with someone who is sick, do community outreach with a nonprofit organization or so much more. You may find great pleasure in doing these things that will glorify God.

DECEMBER 11

ABSORB THE POSITIVE WORDS PEOPLE SAY TO YOU

...If ye have any word of exhortation for the people, say on...

Acts 13:15

God will always place people in your path who will say something positive that will give you a boost for the day. You should absorb those words that are spoken because you may very well have to use what was given to you to share with someone else, or even apply to that situation that you may face today. I once heard, "Words can make you or break you." I am certain you would rather hear positive words over negative words any day. Today, you can start hearing positive words when you surround yourself with people who normally speak positive and carry themselves in a positive manner.

DECEMBER 12

DON'T LET ANYTHING DIVERT YOUR ATTENTION OFF GOD

My heart is fixed...

Psalm 57:7

One thing that we must all remember as Christians is that things will come our way to divert our attention off God. When you have your mind and heart fixed on Jesus, nothing will easily divert your attention from doing His will. Today, I encourage you to stay focused on the things of God.

Don't allow people to come in and impose their opinions and thoughts with the intentions to divert your attention off God. This is all a trick of the enemy, and you have to be on high alert 24 hours a day. He does not want you to do the will of God. He would prefer you work for him. Just keep your heart fixed on God.

DECEMBER 13

SAY I CAN NOT I CAN'T

I can do all things through Christ which strenghteneth me.

Philippians 4:13

There are too many Christians who continue to say "I can't" instead of saying, "I can." The Bible clearly tells us that we can do all things with His strength. Whatever it is that you have been saying that you can't do, I encourage you to start today by saying, "I can pass this test. I can go on a diet. I can get rid of my bad attitude. I can be a good parent (or child). I can respect others. I can write a book. I can start a business. I can start a ministry. I can go back to school to earn my degree. I can buy a home. I can do anything that I want to do as long as I have Jesus Christ with me.

DECEMBER 14

WE ARE SERVING THE LORD IN MY HOUSE

...But as for me and my house, we will serve the Lord

Judges 24:15

The Bible tells us that charity begins at home. With that being said, we must learn to do everything from praying to praising God to worshipping Him to studying His Word to everything in between—right in the comfort of our homes. God is honored when we do these things at home; therefore, we can do them at church as well as other places we go. I encourage you to start serving the Lord in your home, gathering your spouse (if married), your children and start praying this morning before you leave out the door.

DECEMBER 15

YOU WILL FLOURISH

The righteous will flourish like the palm tree...

Psalm 92:12

You are just like "a tree planted by the river," and whether you know it or not, you are flourishing. You are doing something right in your life, and I encourage you to keep going in the direction in which you are taking. God is well-pleased with you. He wants to continue elevating you in all that you do. He has seen your faithfulness, the generosity that you have shown toward others, your humility, your righteousness, and your heart towards Him. He is honored to exalt you to shine in this season of your life. Stand up! "It is your time."

DECEMBER 16

TEACH ME, LORD

Teach me to do thy will...

Psalm 143:10

God wants to teach you His perfect will for your life. Therefore, I encourage you to enjoy being the student as the One instructs you on how to do His will. In order for you to learn from Him, you must yield your heart, mind and soul. He wants to show you how to live Holy. He wants to prepare you for things that you can't see that will come your way. He wants to help you deal with adversity in a godly fashion. He wants to show you how to love those who spitefully use you. Embrace the moment!

DECEMBER 17

LAUNCH OUT

...Launch out into the deep...

Luke 5:4

God wants you to come out of your comfort zone and go out into your community, along the byways and highways, and share the "Good news" with those who have backslidden, those who are at the brink of suicide, those who are in a need of healing, those who are need of shelter, those who need Him, and those who are completed lost. People of God, there is so much work to be done, and because you are an ambassador of Christ, He is calling you to get it done. Today, He wants you to launch out...

DECEMBER 18

GOD REALLY IS JEALOUS

...I the Lord thy God am a jealous God...

Exodus 20:5

Have you been putting your children, your spouse, your mother, your father, your pastor, your job or anything else before God? If so, I want to encourage you to stop today. This is something that God does not like. He wants to be first in all of our lives. If we always put people, places and things before God, He can easily remove everyone and everything we are putting in front of Him to show us that He really means that "He wants it all."

DECEMBER 19

GIVING BIRTH TO YOUR PURPSOSE

Now the birth of Jesus Christ was on the wise...

Matthew 1:18

When a woman gives birth to her child, it is very painful, but by the grace of God so many women have had safe deliveries. I share this to say that you are getting ready to give birth to your purpose, and you may experience pain, but just know that God is right with you. God was with Mary when she gave birth to Jesus Christ—the One who was sent to give His life for us. This was His ultimate purpose.

Each of us has a purpose in life, and many of you are now in the birthing process. I can assure you that you will be happy after you deliver your baby (your purpose), and I guarantee you that God will make sure you have everything you need to nurture it. Enjoy the beginning of your new journey!

DECEMBER 20

YOU LOOK LIKE JESUS

Whosoever believeth that Jesus is Christ is born of God...

1 John 5:1

When you were born, someone said that you looked like either your mother or father or someone else. When your child was born, someone told you that he or she looks like you or the other parent or someone else. When we as Christians accept Jesus Christ as our Lord and Savior, we look just like Him. I want to ask you today, "Do you look like you Jesus?" As a believer, your answer should be "Yes."

There are so many benefits of being a child of God. We are not only beautiful people, but we are given the joy, peace, strength, and everything we need from birth to adults to when we make the transition—to live with Him forever in Heaven.

DECEMBER 21

GOD IS A KEEPER

The Lord is thy keeper...

Psalm 121:5

I have heard people say, "God kept me when I couldn't keep myself." I can assure you that none of us can ever keep ourselves. We definitely need our Heavenly Father to keep us every second, every minute and every hour of each day. I am certain that some of you thought that you could keep yourself, but you found that you didn't have enough strength and had to immediately call on Jesus to pull you out of the mess that you had created. Today, I encourage you to let Jesus keep you. I guarantee you He will keep you from any form of temptations that may be present in your home, on your job, at church, or wherever else you may go this day.

DECEMBER 22

YOUR TOUGH TIMES ARE COMING TO AN END

Wherefore gird up the loins of your mind, be sober, and hope to the end for the grace that is to be brought unto you at the revelation of Jesus Christ.

1Peter 1:13

Today, you can give God a shouting PRAISE! Your tough times are coming to an end. Some of you have had a feeling that something is about to change in your life; that your situation will not be the same. Well, I want to tell you that the unctioning that you have had in your spirit has been confirmed.

You have been fighting with the devil too long; struggling with your finances, and having to endure so much mentally, emotionally, and spiritually. You can be encouraged today, man of God. You can look up, woman of God. You have endured, and God is about to reveal some things to you.

DECEMBER 23

DON'T SAY IT IS TOO DIFFICULT

...Moses spake before the Lord, saying, Behold, the children of Israel have not hearkened unto me; how then shall Pharaoh hear me...?

Exodus 6:12

You may have heard something along the lines of, "It's not hard unless you make it." With that thought, you have to try harder. You can't continue saying that it is too difficult. Whatever that "it" is needs to be eliminated; whether you are saying, "life is difficult, my children are difficult, my job is difficult, my spouse is difficult, this new adventure is difficult, my purpose is difficult and so on. One thing you must realize is that God is not difficult; therefore, with Him on your side, there is nothing too difficult for God to correct.

DECEMBER 24

GOD REJOICES WHEN HE SEES YOU WORKING

Do not despise small beginning, for the Lord rejoices to see the work begin.

Zechariah 4:10 (NLT)

If God gave you a vision and have instructed you to execute, then you just don't need to sit on it. Get up and start working! Don't you know that God rejoices when he sees the work begin? That means He is honored to see you carry out the vision He gave you. We have to be willing to work in His vineyard. There are a lot of lost souls in the world, and believe me, it is your job as a Christian to help win souls. Again, that will require working in His vineyard.

DECEMBER 25

GIVE A NICE GIFT

For God so loved the world, that he gave his only begotten son...

John 3:16

We as Christians have to remember that this day is all about Jesus Christ. God sent Him to give His life for all of us. A very important key word is that He gave. As He freely gave His life, God gave Him power. So as you get out of your bed this morning, think about Jesus Christ, and what He did for you. Give someone a nice gift.

Remember, gifts are not measured by material things. A gift can come in the form of a smile, a hug, a handshake, a card, etc. If you choose to give someone a material gift, then that is good, too. As long as your giving is genuine, I believe that God will smile upon it.

DECEMBER 26

I WILL WAIT

And I will wait upon the Lord...

Isaiah 8:17

The Bible says that those of us who wait on Him shall renew our strength (Isaiah 40:31). That is good news! I have a question for you: Do you mind waiting for God to "show up and show out," pour His blessings upon you, heal your body, calm your fears, make your enemies behave, give you a promotion, and all that He has in store for you? We as children of God must practice waiting on Him.

I want to share that your wait is almost over. You are about to step into your promise land. Yes, the one that God "promised" you. Everything that you have been waiting on and for is about to manifest. Don't give up now. You've been waiting a long time. Someone once told me, "Hang on in there." I pass those very words on to you today.

DECEMBER 27

YOU HAVE IMPROVED

Wherefore he is able to also to save them to the uttermost that come unto God by him, seeing he ever liveth to make intercession for them.

Hebrews 7:25

You can't let anyone tell you that you have not improved. Always remember that God sees and knows where you were, and He sees and knows where you are going. Many of us only judge people based on the old and not the new. When we look at a person through our natural eyes we will only see what is on the surface—the outer person, their past behavior and anything negative about them. Since we all are a "work in progress," we can't really say whether or not a person has improved. The reason being is because God deals with the inner person while we deal with the outer person. This year is coming to a close, and at the beginning of this year, you prayed to God that He helps you to become a better person. Guess what? He has helped you, so you can enjoy the new, improved you. Don't be concerned with what anyone says negative about you. Today, I encourage you to keep growing in the Lord.

DECEMBER 28

I KNEW BONDAGE; I NOW KNOW GOD'S FREEDOM

Lord brought us out...from the house of bondage.

Exodus 13:14

Many of you can attest that you once knew bondage, but you are now experiencing God's freedom. I can surely attest to that. I can also share that it is not a good feeling to be in bondage. It doesn't matter what or who is holding you captive, when you are tired of being in bondage, you will do whatever to get free. I believe that whatever has been holding you captive has to release you. The bondage will end this year. You no longer have to subject yourselves to any type of abuse, struggles, unfruitful friendships or anything else. You can experience God's freedom today.

All you have to do is step right out on faith. The faith that you have, coupled with your desire for freedom, will move you in that direction. You cannot afford to go in any other direction. You have been traveling in the wrong direction way too long. You need to just look back to see exactly how far God has brought you and keep moving forward.

DECEMBER 29

GOD HAS JUSTIFIED IT

...God was manifest in the flesh, justified in the Spirit...

1Timothy 3:16

Some of us have a habit of trying to justify when we do something, whether it is right or wrong. Have you ever done this before? I can say that I have been one of those people who always tried to prove my point, even when I knew that it was all for God's glory. I would give a reason of why I did things and would explain to the max, when I really didn't owe anyone an explanation.

People of God, we should never get to the point of where we feel that we have to explain what God has instructed us to do. Everything we do for Him, He can justify it. There is no need to prove it to anyone else. Just stay committed, stay focused and "run the race that is set before you."

DECEMBER 30

GLORIFY GOD

...Glorify your Father which is in heaven.

Matthew 5:16

Child of God, you should start off today by giving God the glory that belongs to Him. You should not ever go a day without glorifying Him. Give Him the glory for waking you up. Don't even think about stepping foot out of your house without giving Him the glory for your active limbs. He has blessed you to come to the end of the year.

You didn't get here by yourself. Just the thought of that should make you get up right now and shout like crazy. As a matter of fact, He wants the glory, honor, praise and worship.

DECEMBER 31

GET READY FOR YOUR MIRACLE

...He (God) had done so many miracles before them...

John 12:37

One songstress sings, "You are next in line for your miracle." I believe that. If you believe that, then say it, "claim it and receive it." We as Christians know that God can perform many miracles.

Many of you have been seeking a miracle for a long time, and you believe that God is going to drastically change something in your life for the good as we approach a new year. You can go ahead and get ready for your financial miracle. Get ready for your healing miracle! Get ready for your relationship miracle! Get ready for your job miracle! Get ready for your miracle, people of God!

9 780983 322115